A Publication of the

COMMITTEE
FOR MONETARY
RESEARCH & EDUCATION, INC.

Uniform with this Volume

THE
MENACE OF
INFLATION

A Symposium by

Patrick M. Boarman
Lemuel R. Boulware
Yale Brozen
John Chamberlain
Philip M. Crane
Lawrence Fertig
C. Lowell Harriss
Edward C. Harwood
Arthur Kemp
Donald L. Kemmerer
David I. Meiselman
Gary North
Ibrahim M. Oweiss
William Proxmire
Hans F. Sennholz
G. Carl Wiegand

Edited by
G. Carl Wiegand

INFLATION AND UNEMPLOYMENT

Twelve American Economists Discuss
the Unemployment Problem

A Symposium
Edited
and with an
INTRODUCTION
by
G. Carl Wiegand

THE DEVIN-ADAIR COMPANY, *PUBLISHERS*

Old Greenwich, Connecticut

ISBN 0-8159-5825-0
LC Card Catalog Number: 79-55282

Manufactured in the U.S.A.

Canadian Agent: Beaverbooks, Pickering, Ont.

CONTENTS

INTRODUCTION
THE UNEMPLOYMENT PROBLEM
G.C. Wiegand

Since the end of the second World War the struggle for "full employment" has colored, if not determined, public policies in the United States and throughout the free world. According to Senator Wm. Proxmire, unemployment is "the cruelest problem of all problems"; Congressman Hawkins has called unemployment "one of the great moral issues of our times"; and the Humphrey-Hawkins bill of 1976 blamed most of the social ills — "the proliferation of physical and psychological illnesses, drug addiction, crime, and social conflict" — on the "substantial and increasing unemployment."

In Germany, the leader of the Socialists, Helmut Schmidt, campaigned in 1972 under the slogan "rather five percent inflation than five percent unemployment." He won the election and during the subsequent four years the German federal debt increased by 85 percent, the cost of living rose by almost 40 percent — and the rate of unemployment tripled.

This in a country which in 1950 had called for "full employment — but not at any price," and which during the subsequent years warned of "the dangers of the British experiments."

Unemployment is no doubt one of the major problems of our age because of its social and political ramifications, and, above all, because the democratic governments of the West, in their effort to achieve "full employment," tend to undermine the very foundations of the socio-economic system which has created — and is creating — productive jobs on an unprecedented scale. Between 1950 and 1977, the population of the United States grew by about 45 percent, while the number of employed rose by 51 percent. There are more people holding paid — and usually well-paid — jobs today, in relation to the size of the population, than at any time in the nation's history. The present high rate of unemployment is not a symptom of the "collapse of capitalism" or of the "decay of the free society"; — although the efforts of the government to achieve "full employment" at any cost could destroy in the end not only the American economy but individual freedom as well.

Individuals have been unemployed — or underemployed — since the days of the cave dwellers. Europe suffered from chronic underemployment, and periodically from acute unemployment, throughout the 18th and 19th centuries, two centuries of unprecedented economic growth. But there is a fundamental difference between then and now. Past centuries looked upon unemployment and poverty primarily as personal problems which had to be solved through personal efforts, while the modern world regards them as social and political ills which can be cured only through government intervention.

This change in outlook is important.

While it was easier in the 18th and 19th centuries for a man living in a small town or in a rural area to find "some kind of work" to support himself and his family than it is today for the masses of unemployed in the crowded metropolitan centers, the difference between then and now is largely one of degree. Millions of Europeans who found it difficult to make a living in Europe, and had the will to better themselves, emigrated to the United States or other overseas countries, and many of them, or their children, gained affluence. And what is called today "underprivileged youth," those who could not find jobs in New York, were told "go West, young man, go West!"

By thinking of unemployment as a social problem, and thus removing from the individual the immediate responsibility of finding work — any kind of work — to support himself and his family, we have changed the nature of the problem and have created a vast "I-would-work-if" class, millions of unemployed who are willing to "accept" a job, if they "like the type of work," or "if it offers a future" and "pays enough." We are told that "unskilled jobs" are disappearing, while in reality millions of "unemployed" refuse available low-paying jobs, which could be done by marginal workers, as "demeaning" or "substandard."

The 1977 apple crop in Virginia was endangered because of lack of workers, yet 99 per cent of the unemployed in Washington refused to work in the orchards, and in the end the courts ordered the temporary admission of workers from the West Indies to save the crop, while at the same time the "unemployed" in Washington collected unemployment insurance and welfare.

The same situation prevails in Europe. Tens of thousands of German workers are listed as "unemployed," while large numbers of "guest workers" from southern Europe and North Africa do the work which the German workers have come to regard as below their dignity.

Throughout the western world millions of "unemployed"

are perfectly content to live at the expense of "society," that is at the expense of those who work. Some 80 million Americans, who work in industry, commerce and agriculture have to produce enough goods and services to support not only themselves and their families, but in addition more than 15 million government employees, more than two million men and women in the Armed Forces, and six million "unemployed." In other words, every working family of three has to feed a fourth unseen "guest" through direct taxes and/or inflation.

There is no "unemployment" in Russia for two reasons: government red tape causes a tremendous waste of manpower and the would-be unemployed are simply given a broom and told to sweep the streets, or do similar "constructive" work, for which they are paid a purchase-power equivalent of less than $100 a month. In New York, on the other hand, sanitation workers are paid $1000 a month, and periodically go on strike for even higher wages. The results are obvious: the streets in Moscow and Leningrad are a great deal cleaner than in New York and Chicago — and there is no "unemployment" in Russia. At least, there is no statistically defined unemployment.

Nor would there be any unemployment in the United States, if Congress were to adopt similar policies. Given the choice of sweeping the streets for $100 a month or going hungry, even college graduates would prefer the former. But the West has come to regard such a "solution" of the unemployment problem as contrary to "human dignity" and "human rights"; — while the communists proclaim throughout the world that the United States is violating "human rights" by not providing "full employment!"

Unemployment does not exist in two types of societies. In the very primitive household economies where each family produces more or less what it consumes, and consumes what it produces, with a minimum of barter. And in a slave society where the ruler — either the slave owner or the totalitarian state — "puts people to work." Whether we like it or not, the fact remains that unemployment is a sympton of a free society, where the individual has a right to choose whether he wishes to work or not, and what work he is willing to perform, when, where and at what wages.

The totalitarian "solution" of the unemployment problem — forced labor — is obviously impossible in a democracy for ethical as well as for political reasons. The marginal workers who have come to expect an income well above their productive capacity are not only "unemployed," they are also voters who can bring severe pressure on the politicians. And since our age believes that unemployment and poverty are the fault of society rather than of the individual, it seems perfectly logical for society to provide the marginal workers with an income "as if" they had the capacity to support themselves at the same standard of living as fully productive workers.

Unemployed families in New York receive as much as $12,000 in tax-free relief payments, while working families in Kansas have to pay taxes even though they earn less than $12,000 to support the same number of family members. We refuse to face the basic economic and moral dilemma of the philosophy of equalitarianism and welfare-statism which underlies Humphrey-Hawkins Act and all similar make-work schemes. We assume that it is the fault of society that a marginal worker does not earn as much as a fully qualified worker, and that it is hence the responsibility of "society" — those who are trying to make a living through their own efforts — to support the less productive at a standard of living which "society" — or political expediency — regard as "above the poverty level."

The idea is not new, it is not an invention of the second half of the twentieth century. Ancient Rome suffered from chronic and growing unemployment as more and more freed slaves drifted into the major cities, where they were supported by "society." Around the year 200, when the rapid decline of the Roman Empire set in, an estimated 15 percent of the inhabitants of the City of Rome lived, at least in part, on relief; — and the government provided not only "pan" (food) but also "circenses" (mass-entertainment) to keep the voters happy. It may be just a coincidence that in the 1970's, the number of welfare recipients (in the widest sense) in New York City also amounted to about 15 percent.

While Rome was plagued with growing unemployment, Egypt, as far as we know, had no apparent "unemployment problem" for hundreds of years: there were always more pyramids and temples to be built!

Throughout history, every civilization has tried to solve the unemployment problem within the framework of the prevailing social philosophy and political power structure. The 19th century, in the spirit of individualism probably under-estimated the socio-political aspects of unemployment, while our own century of "social conscience" has swung to the opposite extreme, neglecting the primary responsibility of the individual to support himself and his family, and assuming that most social ills will be cured, if only the government can provide everybody with a suitable job.

Until well into the 1930's, unemployment, in the eyes of the American people, involved two aspects. On the one hand, it was a sign of the Calvinist sin of individual laziness — "a man who wants to work can always find some kind of job" — and, on the other, if unemployment produced acute poverty, it called for the exercise of private charity. Throughout the 1930's unemployment remained predominantly an individual problem, even though the New Deal introduced a variety of "emergency" make-work schemes to help the private economy get back on its feet. The "pump-priming" attempt failed. When the war broke out in Europe in 1939, unemployment in the

United States was still at least three times as high as it had been at the end of 1920's, even though the federal government had incurred what was in those days huge deficits, and the national debt had doubled in less than a decade.

But the world learned little from the futility of the New Deal experiment to turn unemployment from a personal into a primarily social problem. It was not during the Great Depression, when at times more than 25 percent of the American labor force was out of work, but during the war years, when the country suffered from an actual labor shortage, that the notion of full employment through government intervention developed. Since then this has become the dominant political creed; a will-o'-the-wisp that threatens to lead the free world into a hopeless economic, political and social guagmire.

What are the premises on which the "full employment" philosophy of the past thirty years rests?

There is first of all the basic socio-political assumption that unemployment is not primarily an individual, but a social problem, and must thus be solved by society as a whole.

Given this assumption, the question arises, how can the goal be achieved. Starting from a partly misinterpreted Keynesian premise, the economists of the 1950's and 1960's argued that unemployment was the result of "inadequate demand" and could thus be overcome if the government provided additional demand through the creation of fiat money. Professor Walter W. Heller, the chief economic advisor of Presidents Kennedy and Johnson, promised that the government would — and could — "provide the essential stability at high levels of employment and growth that the market mechanism, left alone, cannot deliver."

America thus plunged ahead to buy "full employment" through deficit spending and the creation of fiat money. Between 1950 and 1978 federal spending rose from $44 billion to more than $450 billion; the total public debt, federal, state and local, grew from $281 to well over a trillion, and the money supply (currency, demand and time deposits) increased from $183 billion to more than $370 billion. The result of these "stabilization" policies has been — "staglation": between 1950 and 1978 the consumer price index rose from 72 to more than 200, while the number of unemployed grew at times to the highest level since the troubled 1930's.

What went wrong?

The government policies rest upon statistics — so-called "factual data," but, as Professor Parrish points out, many of these statistics contain a strong bias. And, as Professor Sennholz shows, the theoretical assumptions on which the government has been acting are largely misleading. Unemployment is not merely the result of "inadequate demand," the Keynesian thesis, but is caused, as Reed Larson, John Chamberlain and John Q. Jennings show, by workers pricing themselves out of the market as wages rise faster than productivity. Finally, there are the political aspects, the tendency of the government to pursue policies which emphasize consumption at the expense of capital formation.

The future of the country, and of the western world as a whole, may well depend upon the ability of the American people to grasp the true nature of the unemployment problem and to force their leaders to pursue sound long-range policies, even though these may not be popular or politically expedient in the short run.

This book is intended as a contribution toward a better understanding of the critical issue of unemployment and inflation.

I

THE REAL MEANING OF UNEMPLOYMENT STATISTICS

John B. Parrish

Unemployment statistics, at least in the United States, are the most misunderstood of all economic data.

It has been said, again and again, U.S. unemployment is "shockingly" high when compared to other advanced industrial countries.

It is said, U.S. teenage unemployment is "frightening," "disgraceful," "alarming," and a "seething time bomb ready to explode."

It is said, "high and sticky" overall domestic unemployment reflects the deteriorating ability of the free enterprise system to create enough jobs for all who seek them.

During his 1976 campaign, President Carter, repeated again and again that U.S. unemployment was "distressing" and "much too high." It was the nation's No. 1 economic and social problem. It represented the failure of the economic system in general, and the policies of the previous Administration, in particular. This repeated assertion may well have won him the Presidency.

These claims are simply not true, and this essay will try to explain *why* they are not true.

I shall concentrate on just six aspects: first, international unemployment comparisons as reported in official statistics; second, the real meaning of these international comparisons; third, the special problem of U.S. youth unemployment; fourth, the unusual behavior of employment and unemployment in the recession and recovery, 1974-1976; fifth, some institutional factors tending to raise long run unemployment rates in this country, and sixth the changing role of women in the U.S. labor force.

UNEMPLOYMENT IN THE U.S. AND IN OTHER INDUSTRIAL COUNTRIES

Measured by officially reported statistics, and adjusted to U.S. concepts, the data do indicate that, since the end of World War II, unemployment has been very much higher in the U.S. than in other countries.

For example, over the years 1959-1975, unemployment averaged under two percent in Sweden, Australia, Japan and West Germany. It averaged 2.4 percent in France, 3.1 percent in the United Kingdom, about 4 percent in Italy. But in the U.S., the overall rate averaged 5.2 percent, exceeded only by Canada's 5.4 percent.

Thus the relative inferior performance of the U.S. (and Canada) appears confirmed by the official statistics.

However, a careful examination of the statistical details reveals that the use of overall unemployment rates for comparative purposes, is somewhat misleading. Let's look at the data by age groups.

In the primary working years, 25 to 54 years of age, the unemployment rate over the years 1968-1974, averaged a very low 3.2 percent in the U.S. By any standard of measurement this is a very satisfactory and acceptable rate. The rates for this same age group in eight other industrial countries ranged from a low of 1.0 percent in Japan to a high of 3.3 percent in Great Britain and 3.9 percent in Canada.

Similarly a comparison of unemployment among senior workers, 55 years of age and over, reveals the U.S. compares very favorably with the other countries. The rate for this age group was 2.6 percent for the U.S., which was considerably lower than the rate of 7.3 percent in Australia, 4.3 percent in Canada, 3.6 percent in Great Britain, and very little above the rates of 2.4 percent for France and 1.9 percent for Sweden.[2]

The reason for the elevated overall U.S. unemployment rate, relative to other countries, is thus due primarily to the unusually high unemployment among U.S. teenagers and young adults.

The statistics bear this out. U.S. teenage unemployment, 1968-1974 averaged 15 percent. This contrasts with 5.0 percent in Australia, 7.3 percent in France, 2.5 percent in West Germany, 2.3 percent in Japan and 5.6 percent in Sweden. The same very wide differentials are reported for young adults, 20 to 24 years of age. The average rate for the U.S. for this age group was 7.7 percent in contrast to 2.2 percent in Australia, 3.7 percent in France, 1.0 percent in West Germany, 2.0 percent in Japan and 2.9 percent in Sweden.

HOW TO EXPLAIN THE INTERNATIONAL UNEMPLOYMENT DIFFERENTIALS

How does one explain the international differentials in unemployment rates, particularly among teenagers and young adults?

There are two possible explanations. One is differences in concepts and methods of measurement. The other is differences in the institutional setting.

The first possible explanation, i.e., differences in methods of data collection and concepts, can be, in general, ruled out. It is fair to conclude that the U.S. Bureau of Labor Statistics has done a competent professional job in adjusting the data of other countries to U.S. methodology and concepts.[3] Whatever methodological differences remain, may be considered minor.

The explanation for the differences must therefore be sought in the institutional settings and labor market dynamics.

WHY ARE UNEMPLOYMENT FIGURES HIGHER IN THE U.S. THAN IN OTHER COUNTRIES?

There are at least seven major factors which account for the relatively high U.S. unemployment rates compared with other industrial countries.

First, is the sharp difference in the length of transition from school to job. In the U.S. the transition is long. In all other countries it comes early in the life of youth and is very short. In fact, school to job may be coterminous.

In 1970, nearly 40 percent of U.S. youth was still in school. The percentages for other countries were: Japan, 14 percent; United Kingdom, 9; Italy, 5; Sweden, 20; France, 15; Canada, 24; West Germany, 8. During the long U.S. transition, youth make frequent moves in and out of the labor force. When they seek jobs, they usually seek part-time jobs that will fit into school schedules. This makes for relatively high unemployment rates. In other countries youth leave school much earlier, at around 15 or 16 years of age. They move into the labor force, full time and for life. This obviously makes for much lower unemployment rates.

Although the U.S. transition pattern results in elevated unemployment rates compared to other countries, it also reflects greater educational opportunities, greater opportunities for job tryout, greater opportunities to mature and to make better final career choices. To this extent, high U.S. youth unemployment rates are favorable, not unfavorable; constructive over time, not wasteful. They represent a high degree of freedom of choice, not a tightly restricted choice.[4]

Second, there are very sharp differences between the U.S. and other countries in the attitude of youth, parents and employers toward youth employment. As noted above, in other countries, youth leave school early for full time, full life employment and this commitment involves strong loyalty to the original employer. In turn, the employer agrees to train youth with the expectancy of a lifetime of employment regardless of whether a youth's employment is currently needed. This early employer-youth apprenticeship arrangement is backed up, not only by strong social custom, but often by youth-parent-employer contracts, legally enforceable in the courts. The result: much disguised unemployment, but very low reported turnover rates and unemployment.

No such social arrangements exist in the U.S. Youth take jobs and readily leave them. Employers expect high turnover rates among teenagers. The result: relatively high youth unemployment. Once again, however, it must be noted, that while there is considerable lost time and wastage in the U.S. process, there is also much that is positive in terms of job tryout, freedom to earn money with which to continue education, freedom to explore opportunities and a chance to enjoy an extended youth period. [5]

Third, the differences cited above are reinforced by sharp differences in the entry wages of youth in the U.S. compared with other countries.

In all the other eight industrial countries, youth enter industry at wages far below prevailing adult rates. Foreign employers are willing to hire youth because it costs them so little for so many months. No such "youth rates" exist in the U.S. Here, employers must pay the federal minimum, which, when fringe benefits were added probably amounted to $3.25 to $3.50 an hour in 1976. In 1977 minimum wages and fringe benefits were raised further, even though President Carter himself admitted that the higher minimum wages make far more unemployment among the young and the marginal workers.

There is no doubt that the high entry wage rates for youth in the U.S. discourages the employment of teenagers. Or, to put the matter differently, much youth unemployment in this country is created by the federal wage minimum, which the AFL-CIO is trying to push still higher and higher.

Fourth, there are very important differences in layoff policies in the U.S. as contrasted with other countries. Foreign employers are under very great social and governmental pressure, not to lay off workers even in slack times. The result is much disguised unemployment abroad that does not show up in the official unemployment statistics. U.S. employers are under no such pressures. When workers are not needed they are laid off and counted among the unemployed. In the great auto slump in Detroit in 1975-1976, thousands of senior workers exercised their seniority rights to be laid off and let the junior workers continue on the job. Why? Because they could obtain about 90 percent of regular income while not working. The State of Michigan reported sending thousands of unemployment compensation checks to Florida every month.

Fifth, teenagers are a larger proportion of the U.S. population than in other countries. Since youths have higher unemployment rates in this country than do adults, this fact tends to elevate our overall unemployment rate. In 1970 the percent of the U.S. population under 15 years of age was 29 percent. The percentages for the other industrial countries (Canada excepted) ranged from 25 percent in France down to

21 percent in Sweden.[5]

Sixth, there are differences in labor force growth rates. Other things being equal it is self-evident that a country with a rapidly growing labor force will have higher rates of unemployment than countries with very slow rates of growth or declining labor forces. During the years 1959-1974 the annual U.S. labor force growth rate was relatively rapid, a little over 2 percent, exceeded only by Canada and Australia. The growth rate was 1.0 percent in France, 0.5 percent in Great Britain, 1.3 percent in Japan and 0.8 percent in Sweden. The labor force actually declined 0.3 percent annually in West Germany and 0.4 percent in Italy.[6]

One of the major factors holding down unemployment in the U.S., despite the rapid growth in the labor force, has been the outstanding performance of the U.S. economy in creating new jobs. In the difficult years 1970-1974 employment grew faster in the U.S. than in any of nine other industrial countries, Canada excepted. Using 1970 as 100, the employment index for the U.S. in 1974 was 109 in contrast to 101 for Japan, 103 for Sweden, 102 for United Kingdom and a decline to 98 for West Germany.[7]

Seventh, while in the U.S. government policies tend to expose unemployment many other industrial countries try to hide it. Total job security is woven into the employer-employee relationship in most of these countries. A Swedish employer who wants to cut back on his work force must justify his decision before a labor market board, two months in advance. In France an employer who wishes to cut back his work force must, by law, consult with a workers' council in advance. He can count on vigorous opposition. In Italy, an employer is discouraged by law from dismissing a worker, or even remaining neutral if the worker voluntarily quits, by a legal requirement according to which he must pay a worker a stiff "seniority indemnity."

In Belgium, in 1976, the government required all firms and government agencies with 100 or more employees to expand their payroll by 1 percent to create jobs for workers up to age 30, regardless of whether the employer had any need for such workers. At the other end of the life span the Belgium government provides a "solidarity fund" to give workers 80 percent of normal take-home pay until they reach the standard pension age of 65 for men, 60 for women. When older workers retire under this plan, one employee under 30 must be hired regardless of whether needed. In Sweden, in the 1973 cyclical downturn, 98,000 workers were officially counted as unemployed. This compares with 80,000 enrolled in training programs or employed on public work projects. The 80,000 were considered employed, not unemployed. Thus 45 percent of the Swedish unemployed was hidden. In West Germany, foreign workers have made up ten percent of the civilian labor force in recent years. In slack times they don't become Germany's unemployed. They are simply sent home.

All these, and many other forms of government actions abroad, make for seemingly low unemployment rates, compared with the U.S.[8]

The evidence thus supports the following conclusions. International comparisons, which report U.S. unemployment rates much higher than in most other industrial countries, are inappropriate. The comparative labor market conditions are so different as to make comparisons misleading. If one could place U.S. market conditions into the other countries, it is a reasonable guess unemployment rates would be higher abroad than in the U.S.

U.S. teenage unemployment is not destructive and "grim." Much of it is constructive and is, or should be, the envy of teenagers around the world.

THE SPECIAL PROBLEM OF U.S. YOUTH UNEMPLOYMENT

Because of the importance of the relatively high U.S. youth unemployment, and the fact it has been so widely misunderstood and misinterpreted, it is helpful to expand somewhat on what recent research tells us about it.

In 1975 the annual unemployment rate for adults, 35 years of age and over, was around 5 percent. The rate for all teenagers, 16 to 17 years of age, was reported as 22 percent. And among black teenagers, in this age class, the rate was around 40 percent.[9] The latter does indeed sound "horrendous" and "grim."

Teenagers are only about 10 percent of the labor force but they account for about 25 percent of the unemployed.[10] About half of all "unemployed" teenagers are still in school, which obviously limits their job search and the kinds of jobs they can accept. Since most of these teenagers must find part-time jobs, this prolongs job search and raises their unemployment rates.

In evaluating the nature of youth unemployment it is important to keep two aspects in mind.

First, most U.S. youth unemployed are *not job losers*. In October 1976, for instance, there were 1,600,000 teenagers reported as unemployed. Of these, 10 percent were voluntary job leavers, 30 percent were reentrants, 40 percent were new entrants, and only 20 percent were job losers.[11]

Second, there is abundant research evidence available to support the conclusion that, despite the barrier which may be imposed by mandated minimum wages, youth who complete schooling and who seek full-time jobs, do find these jobs and they find reasonably good jobs.[12] Many of these jobs, probably most, are not dead-end jobs. Rather they are jobs with relatively high entry pay which offer a clearcut line of upward progression. Despite this, voluntary turnover rates among youth workers remains high.[13] The widespread reports of discrimination, "floundering around," the inability of youth to find jobs "because of the decline in low skill jobs usually filled by youth," all these are, as one able scholar put it, "part of the folk lore about youth unemployment,"[14] or as another scholar puts it, the high unemployment rates of teenagers is "not due to inability to find jobs — it is due to their inability to stay on the jobs."

If the above explanation for high U.S. youth unemployment is approximately correct, then current proposals to spend billions to provide youth jobs in public services, or more training programs, may well turn out to be ineffective in reducing youth unemployment. In fact they could prove wasteful and counterproductive if youth take on the easy "welfare" jobs and postpone serious job search and training. Eighteen years of massive federal expenditures on youth programs have produced minimal results. In fact, as federal expenditures have risen, so has teenage unemployment. This should tell reasonable men something about the nature of the problem. But then there is always the fact that political expediency is likely to win out over reason.

SOME FACTORS TENDING TO RAISE UNEMPLOYMENT RATES

What are the factors which tend to raise unemployment rates in this country?

First, an increasing proportion of U.S. unemployment is voluntary as a result of the steady rise in the holdout power of workers. This holdout power has many different sources. The liberalization of unemployment compensation benefits, to the point that some workers can get 75 to 100 percent of normal wages while not working, has lengthened job search and encouraged some employers to lay off workers.[15] The liberalization of welfare benefits has reached the point in some big cities that welfare income is higher, and much more certain, than income from working.[16] A rapid rise in the percent of families with several wage earners has given families much more holdout power. In 1900 only 6 percent of U.S. families were multi-worker. By 1950 the rate was 36 percent and by 1975 it had reached 49 percent. Among husband-wife families, 55 percent were in the multi-earner category in 1975.

The implications are considerable. For example, in the first quarter of 1976 there were 7.2 million unemployed, of which 6.9 million, or 95.8 percent, were members of family groups. About 68 percent of the 6.9 million had at least one other relative in the family who was employed. This obviously cushioned the blow of unemployment.[17] Or to put it differently, most recent U.S. jobless persons have working relatives.

In the distant past, unemployment usually caused immediate hardship for families. Unemployment statistics were, in that sense, "hard." This is less and less true today. Unemployment statistics are becoming soft and less and less meaningful, because they reflect less and less hardship. This may be demonstrated by the fact that unemployment is disappearing as a cause of poverty. In 1959, 34 percent of all families with the head unemployed were in poverty. By 1974 the ratio had fallen to just 16 percent.[18]

A second factor tending to elevate unemployment is the changing composition of the labor force. By sex and age group, the lowest unemployment rates are found among males 25 years of age and older. As a percent of the labor force this group has declined from 59.8 percent in 1955 to 46.9 percent in 1975. Females, 25 years of age and older, have unemployment rates from 20 to 50 percent higher than men in the same age class. Women, 25 years of age and over, have increased as a percent of the labor force, from 25 percent in 1955 to 29 percent in 1975. The highest unemployment rates are those of both sexes. Their rates run two to three times higher than for the older adult workers. Teenagers as a percent of the labor force have risen from 6.3 percent in 1955 to 9.5 percent in 1975. Thus, the increasing proportion of the labor force made up of women and teenagers, have in the past, and will continue in the future, to elevate the overall national unemployment rate.[19] One of the reasons for this is that women and teenagers have high rates of part-time employment and part-time workers have higher rates of unemployment. In 1974, 13 percent of men worked part-time, 32 percent of women. The average unemployment rates, 1963-1974 for full-time workers was 4.4 percent. For part-time workers it was 7.4 percent. About 70 percent of the teenagers who worked in 1974, worked part-time.[20] The percent of the labor force working part-time has been rising and may be expected to continue to rise in the future.

Another factor tending to raise unemployment rates is the hidden and largely unreported, but enormous, number of immigrant workers holding jobs, many of which would otherwise be held by American citizens. No one knows for certain the actual annual increase in the size of the illegal immigrant force, but the following official estimates give some idea of the magnitude of the problem:[21]

Estimated Annual Number of Alien Persons Entering the United States in 1976

Illegal immigrants	
Illegal visitor overstays	300,000
Illegal student overstays	93,000
Illegal alien migrant workers	500,000
Total illegal alien persons	893,000
Legal immigrants	200,000
Total illegal and legal immigrants	1,093,000

Between 1971 and 1976 an estimated three to five million illegal aliens joined the American labor force. Of these eight out of ten were employed, but do not answer to official household enumeration surveys. If we assume a minimum of three million illegal job holders, unemployment could well be down to 3-4 million, or about four percent, if the illegal workers were removed and American workers hired to take their place. However, since there are no immediate prospects for stopping the stream of illegal aliens into this country, primarily from Mexico, one can only conclude this illegal labor force will continue to raise U.S. unemployment rates, perhaps by as much as 20 to 40 percent.

A fourth factor tending to raise reported unemployment has been the decline in the proportion of the unemployed who are either self-employed or unpaid members in a family enterprise. As a percent of all employed they have declined from 21.5 in 1948 to 9.7 in 1975. Both groups typically report very low unemployment, presumably because their earnings are residual and not contractual. For example in 1975 the unemployment rate for these two groups was about one percent and the rate for all experienced workers 8.5 percent.[22]

A fifth factor which contributes to higher unemployment rates is the high and rising cost of hiring new workers, due to rising fringe benefits. These include employer contributions to Social Security, private pension plans, insurance, paid vacations, paid sick leave, profit sharing, unemployment compensation, and other benefits. In 1975 average pay for time worked in industry was $9,709. The cost of fringe benefits was $3,984 for a total of $13,693 with the fringe benefits accounting for 30 percent of the total. In many industries the fringes account for over 35 percent of employee costs.[23] As a consequence, private concerns are finding it more economical to work the existing labor force overtime than to hire new workers, thus adding to unemployment levels.

A sixth factor tending to elevate U.S. unemployment rates is the rising divorce and separation rates. This country has the highest divorce rate in the world. It reached 4.8 per 1,000 population in 1975, double the rate of a decade ago. The rate of 4.8 percent contrasts with rates of 3.1 for Sweden, 2.4 in the United Kingdom, rates of around 1 percent in West Germany, Australia, Japan and France, and 0.3 in Italy.[24]

In March 1975, 12.3 percent of the U.S. female labor force was either divorced or separated, up from 10.7 in 1970. This rise elevates overall unemployment rates simply because divorced or separated women are more likely to be unemployed. A special study in 1974 reported the unemployment rates as follows: women married, husband present, 8.7 percent; divorced, 14.8 percent; separated, 18.3 percent.[25]

A seventh institutional factor contributing somewhat to the high and rising U.S. unemployment rates is the growing number of births among teenage women. Among 22 countries ranked from high to low in teenagers' fertility rates, the U.S. was fourth from the top. Of the 600,000 teenage women who gave birth in 1974, at least 60 percent were unwillingly pregnant. One third were not married, and this rate has been rising. And studies show that teenage mothers have much higher unemployment rates than women who first give birth after the age of 20. This process perpetuates itself. Research studies report that the children of teenage mothers, when they reach their teens, are much more likely to have high rates of unemployment, delinquency, dependency on welfare, than are children of women who postpone child bearing until after the age of 20. To the extent that liberalized welfare policies encourage low income teenagers to carry pregnancies to term, the federal government has been a major factor in creating this source of unemployment.[26]

An eighth factor tending to elevate unemployment rates in this country is the very heavy cost of government regulation.

It is impossible to make precise estimates of these costs. The steel industry reports it will be spending over $1 billion a year for many years for pollution controls alone. EPA estimates it will cost industry between 1978 and 1985 about $60 billion for capital equipment and another $12 billion for operating and maintenance costs just to meet 1963 water pollution standards. It is estimated that it will cost at least $15 billion in capital costs to meet OSHA's noise standards. Other estimates indicate industry will have to spend up to $112 billion in 1972-1981 to meet all types of pollution standards.

Won't the expenditure of all these billions create jobs and to that extent lessen unemployment? Irving Kristol has been quick to point out that one must distinguish between "capital spending" and "capital investing," between creating jobs by building pyramids or building new, more efficient production facilities.[27] In 1976, capital investment was reported as $121 billion. But Professor Kristol calls attention to the fact that at least 10 percent of this, perhaps more, consisted of economically unproductive expenditures to meet government regulations which leaves us with a net reduction from 1975 in true capital investment. This could continue for many years, and could prove to be a tremendous drag on the productive job-creating ability of the free enterprise system keeping unemployment artificially high. Because of delays in getting approval, because of arbitrary and capricious rejection of construction proposals by federal courts and agencies, there are billions of dollars worth of needed projects now collecting dust in business files. Here again, the cost in unemployment is likely to be high. To the extent that it is, it is government created unemployment.

CONCLUSIONS AND COMMENTS

Employment and unemployment statistics — what do they mean?

In comparing U.S. unemployment with that of other industrial countries, the statistics mean very little without careful interpretation. Given the latter, U.S. unemployment is probably no higher than abroad, and, if one could equate labor market conditions, might well be lower.

Relatively high U.S. youth unemployment rates are one of the most misinterpreted of all labor market data. The description of U.S. youth unemployment as "grim," "disgraceful," "horrendous" by many labor economists some in high places, is open to serious question. Much U.S. youth unemployment serves a useful purpose and reflects the advantages of a free labor market. The youth market needs greater efficiency and information but is not a "time bomb waiting to explode."

FOOTNOTES

1. Unpublished data, Productivity and Technology Division, Bureau of Labor Statistics, U.S. Department of Labor, February 15, 1977.
2. Arithmetic mean, 1968, 1970, 1974, for all countries, except 1968 and 1970 for France, 1968, 1970, 1972 for Italy, and the single year of 1971 for Great Britain. Source: Unpublished data, Productivity and Technology Division, Bureau of Labor Statistics, U.S. Department of Labor, February 15, 1977.
3. For a discussion of the technical aspects of international comparisons see: Janet L. Norwood, "Problems Involved in Making International Unemployment Comparisons," prepared statement before hearings on *Employment-Unemployment*, Joint Economic Committee, U.S. Congress, 94th, 2d Session, Part 7, June 4, 1976, pp. 1314-1315; Constance Sorrentino, "Unemployment in the United States and Seven Foreign Countries," *Monthly Labor Review*, Vol. 93, No. 9, September 1970, pp. 18-22; Joyanna Moy and Constance Sorrentino, "Unemployment in Nine Industrial Countries 1973-75," *Monthly Labor Review*, Vol. 98, No. 6, June 1976, pp. 9-18; President's Committee to Appriase Employment and Unemployment Statistics, *Measuring Employment and Unemployment*,

GPO, Washington, D.C. 1962; "Students in Labor Force: An International Comparison for Major Countries" Unpublished manuscript from Office of Productivity and Technology (Jerome A. Mark, Assistant Commissioner) Bureau of Labor Statistics, U.S. Department of Labor, Washington, D.C.; Robert J. Myers and John H. Chandler, "International Comparisons of Unemployment" *Monthly Labor Review*, August 1962, pp. 857-864, September 1962, pp. 969-974.

4. OECD (Organization for Economic Co-Operation and Development) *Educational Statistics Yearbook*, Vol. II, Paris, 1975.

5. OECD (Organization for Economic Cooperation and Development), *Demographic Trends in OECD Countries, 1970-1985*, Paris, 1976.

6. Constance Sorrentino, "Unemployment in Nine Industrial Countries," *Monthly Labor Review*, Vol. 95, No. 6, June 1972, p. 30;
_____ , Vol. 98, No. 6, June 1975, p. 12.

7. International Labour Office, *ILO Yearbook of Labour Statistics, 1975.*

8. Council of Economic Advisers, Annual Report of the President, February 1975, pp. 98-102; President's Committee to Appraise Employment and Unemployment Statistics, Measuring Employment and Unemployment Statistics, Measuring Employment and Unemployment Statistics, Measuring Employment and Unemployment, Washington, D.C., GPO, 1962; Business Week, October 17, 1964, p. 45; A. H. Raskin, "the System Keeps the Young Waiting," New York Times, December 5, 1976; Beatrice G. Reubens, "Foreign and American Experience With the Youth Transition," Ch. 10 in *From School to Work: Improving the Transition.* A Collection of Policy Papers Prepared for the National Commission for Manpower Policy, The Commission, Washington, D.C., 1976, pp. 273-294; Franz Groemping, "Transition from School to Work" in *Princeton Man-Power Symposium*, May 1968 (Princeton: Industrial Relations Section, Princeton University, Research Report Series No. 111, 1968), pp. 132088; David Bauer, *Factors Moderating Unemployment Abroad, The Conference Board*, Studies in Business Economics, No. 113, New York, 1970; Organization for Economic Cooperation and Development, *The Entry* of Youth into Working Life, 1975; European Economic Community, *Measures to Reduce Youth Unemployment*, Brussels, May 1975; Council of Europe, *Unemployment Among Young People and Its Social Aspects* Strasbourg, 1975; "The Problem of Young People's Entry into Working Life," *OECD Observer*, September-October, 1975, pp. 14-16.

9. *Employment and Training Report of the President, 1976*, pp. 241-243.

10. Diane Westcott, "Youth in the Labor Force: An Area Study," *Monthly Labor Review*, Vol. 99, No. 7, July 1976, pp. 3-9.

11. *Employment and Earnings*, U.S. Department of Labor, November 1976,

Table A-14. For an extended discussion of this subject see: Curtis L. Gilroy, "Job Losers, Leavers and Entrants: Traits and Trends," *Monthly Labor Review*, Vol. 96, No. 8, August 1973, pp. 3-15.

12. Stephen Marston, in *Brookings Papers on Economic Activity*, No. 1, 1976, pp. 200-203.

13. *From School to Work: Improving the Transition.* A Collection of Policy Papers Prepared for the National Commission for Manpower Policy, Ch. 3, "Corporate Hiring Practices," Washington, D.C., 1975, pp. 37-42.

14. Hugh Folk, "The Problem of Youth Unemployment," in *The Transition from School to Work*, The Princeton Manpower Symposium, Princeton, New Jersey, 1968, pp. 76-107.

15. Martin Feldstein, "Unemployment Compensation, Its Effect on Unemployment, *Monthly Labor Review*, Vol. 99, No. 3, March 1976, pp. 39-41; _____ "Unemployment Compensation: Adverse Incentives and Distribution Anomalies," *National Tax Journal*, June 1974; _____The Importance of Temporary Layoffs: An Empirical Analysis," in *Brookings Papers on Economic Activity*, No. 3, 1975; _____ "Temporary Layoffs in the Theory of Unemployment," *Journal of Political Economy*, June 1976; Ronald G. Ehrenberg and Ronald L. Oaxaca, "Do Benefits Cause Unemployed to Hold Out for Better Jobs?," *Monthly Labor Review*, Vol. 99, No. 3, March 1976, pp. 37-39; National Taxpayers Union, release of December 1976; Paul L. Burgess and Jerry L. Kingston, "The Impact of Unemployment Insurance Benefits on Reemployment Success," *Industrial and Labor Relations Review*, Vol. 30, No. 1, October 1976, pp. 25-31 (contains excellent summary of the literature, footnote 2, p. 25).

16. E.g., a recent study of welfare families in Los Angeles reported a typical AFDC family, headed by an unemployed father and including four children, was entitled to monthly welfare benefits of $447, consisting of $282 cash, $80 worth of food stamps, $85 worth of medical and dental care, tax free. It was estimated the father would have to earn $626 a month at $3.61 an hour or $7,515 a year to equal the net welfare benefits he would have received without working. The average wage obtained by those men who went through the WIN (Work Incentive Program) training program and found work was $3.15 an hour, $546 a month, or $6,549 a year. This latter income, after taxes and work related expenses, was $65 a month less than the value of the welfare benefits the family would have received if the father had not worked. Source: *Problems in Accomplishing Objectives of the Work Incentive Program*, U.S. General Accounting Office, September 24, 1971. By 1975, the liberalized AFDC payments to families with unemployed fathers had been extended to 23 states and the District of Columbia. Source: *Annual Report of the Council of Economic*

Advisers, 1975, p. 96. That it pays to remain unemployed on welfare rather than work is supported by much research evidence.

17. Howard Hayghe, "Families and the Rise of Working Wives — an Overview," *Monthly Labor Review*, Vol. 99, No. 5, May 1976, pp. 12-19; Howard Hayghe, "New Data Series on Families Shows Most Jobless Have Working Relatives," *Monthly Labor Review*, Vol. 99, No. 12, p. 46.

18. U.S. Bureau of the Census, Current Population Reports, Series P-60, early issues and No. 102, p. 91.

19. *Employment and Training Report of the President, 1977.* See also Geoffrey H. Moore, *How Full is Full Employment*, American Enterprise Institute for Public Policy Research, Washington, D.C., July 1973, p. 28.

20. *Guide to Consumer Markets, 1975-76*, U.S. Department of Labor, 1976; *Worker Experience of the Population in 1974*, Special Labor Force Report, June 1975, U.S. Department of Labor; *Employment and Training Report of the President, 1976; Handbook of Labor Statistics 1975*, U.S. Department of Labor, p. 145.

21. *Immigration — Need to Reassess U.S. Policy.* Report to the Congress by the Comptroller of the United States, October 12, 1976, *Immigrants and the American Labor Market. Manpower Administration*, Research Monograph No. 31, U.S. Department of Labor, 1974.

22. *Annual Report of the Council of Economic Advisers, 1975*, p. 97; Employment and Training Report of the President, 1976, p. 244.

23. *U.S. News and World Report*, October 25, 1976, p. 83.

24. *Demographic Yearbook 1974*, United Nations, New York, 1976.

25. Allyson Sherman Grossman, "The Labor Force Patterns of Divorced and Separated Women," *Monthly Labor Review*, Vol. 100, No. 1, January 1977, pp. 48-53.

26. *11 Million Teenagers.* Alan Guttmacher Institute, New York, 1976.

27. Irving Kristol, "The Hidden Costs of Regulations," *The Wall Street Journal*, January 12, 1977. See also the editorial "Heroes of the Movement," the *Journal*, February 22, 1977.

II

THE CRISIS OF KEYNESIANISM

Hans F. Sennholz

After almost forty years of smooth sailing in academic and political waters, the Keynesian ship has run aground. It is taking water and is beginning to break up. Massive rescue operations to free the giant tanker are continuing, but the chances of success are small, and there is growing concern about the pollution that will follow the wreck.

The Keynesian ship is stranded on two rocks, inflation and unemployment, and the Keynesians are calling for help and are offering rich rewards to potential rescuers. Paul A. Samuelson even holds up the hope of a Nobel Prize to the brave deliverer. "No jury of expert economists," he comments, "can agree on a satisfactory solution for the modern disease of 'stagflation', and many of the proffered cures may be as bad as the disease itself. That is why one can say that some young economist can win for herself or himself a Nobel Prize on the basis of an empirical or theoretical breakthrough that will help the mixed economy cope better with the present-day scourge."[1]

Modern inflation, the Keynesians lament, differs from that of the past in that prices and wages continue to rise while there is underemployment of capital and labor. When the monetary and fiscal brakes are applied and the rate of cost-push inflation, especially the rise in wages in excess of the increase in productivity, is limited, the managed economy sinks into a deep recession. Without the brakes, the inflation accelerates while unemployment remains high or even rises. The Keynesian model C + I + G (Consumption plus Investments plus Government Spending), which if properly manipulated was expected to assure monetary stability plus full employment, has lost its magic power.

And the Phillips Curve, which was hailed as the macromanagers' blueprint, has become a big question mark. Its quantification of the trade-off relationship between unemployment and wage rates obviously is more fiction than description. And its pictorial message that a low rate of inflation means high unemployment, and greater inflation less unemployment, is spurious. The fact is that the Keynesian formula of full employment through monetary and fiscal stimulation is finally yielding its foreseeable results: rising rates of inflation together with growing unemployment.

The Keynesian system contains many errors, too numerous to analyze in this essay. But we must mention just a few that have a bearing on the problem of unemployment. In particular, we must reject the basic psychological maxim that government can fool all the people all the time.

POOR PSYCHOLOGY

Lord Keynes was relying on the economic ignorance of wage earners and their union agents. Since unions will not accept a reduction in wage rates, Keynes suggested deficit spending and credit expansion by the government to produce rising prices, which, he argued, would automatically lower real wages and thus increase employment; provided, of course, that wages did not rise at the same rate as prices. No doubt, lower real wages tend to raise the demand for labor and reduce unemployment. But the success of the Keynesian plan depends entirely on the ability to deceive the workers and their unions, or, if this should fail, to persuade them to suffer voluntary losses in real income.

Deceit is always the false road to a solution. It weaves a tangled web, which in the end misleads the user and destroys the confidence of others. While the Keynesians are weaving, the workers are marching in picket lines. They need no Ph.D. in Keynesian economics to understand how rising prices reduce the purchasing power of their income. They are quick to demand wage boosts that compensate for the rise in goods prices, and they may force rises in money wage rates that anticipate future purchasing power losses lest they lose during the life of the contract. Both demands, designed to protect workers against the effects of inflation together with the additional demand for higher real incomes because of "rising labor productivity," are foiling the Keynesian scheme.

The post-Keynesians now admit that the customary dosages of monetary and fiscal policy no longer cause real wages to adjust to provide full employment. They speak of a great discovery of a new type of inflation in which labor does not want to be deceived, but continues to push for higher wages regardless of the recipe. In frustration and desperation, the Keynesian professors are developing new theories on "cost-push inflation" and charting new curves that are to explain the dilemma. Abraham Lincoln already answered the Keynesian cunning: "You cannot fool all of the people all of the time."

Because economic reality does not conform to their doctrines, Keynesians now are joining many utopians and would-be reformers, urging the use of force to fit man into their peculiar mold. To force economic life into the Keynesian mold they are debating the use of government force. Wanted:

an incomes policy, i.e., wage and price controls, or governmental guideposts, or government getting tough with the unions, or some other force of deliverance.

INSTITUTIONAL UNEMPLOYMENT

All presidents, from FDR to Jimmy Carter, have initiated programs for full employment. They all pledged top priority to the problem of mass unemployment. And yet, except for the World War II years, unemployment has been our constant companion ever since 1930. In fact, the problem seems to grow ever more acute as it now makes its ugly appearance even in boom times. About seven million Americans — and according to AFL-CIO statistics more than ten million — were looking for jobs in 1977 although the economy was said to be prosperous and growing.

The Carter Administration, like all others before it, is not really coping with the causes of unemployment. Under the influence of post-Keynesian conceptions it seeks once again to stimulate the economy through deficit spending and credit expansion, through tax rebates and public works, and by raising minimum wages and increasing unemployment compensation: the very measures that create unemployment rather than alleviate it.

Throughout the Keynesian and post-Keynesian era the inexorable laws of economics have not changed. Unemployment still is, and always has been, a cost phenomenon. A worker whose employment adds valuable output and is profitable to his employer can always find a job. A worker whose employment inflicts losses is destined to be unemployed. As long as the earth is no paradise there is an infinite amount of work to be done. But if a worker produces only $2 per hour while the government decrees a minimum wage of $2.90 an hour plus sizeable fringe costs, he cannot be employed. For a businessman to hire him would mean capital loss and waste. In other words, any compulsion, be it by government or union, to raise labor costs above those determined by the marginal productivity of labor, creates institutional unemployment.

UNEMPLOYMENT AND PSEUDO-HUMANITARIANISM

The problems of unemployment are badly obscured by popular pseudo-humanitarianism according to which the demand for higher labor costs is a noble demand for the improvement of the conditions of the working man. Politicians and labor leaders who forcibly raise labor costs parade as the only true friends of labor and the "common man," and as the only stalwarts of progress and social justice. Actually, they are causing mass unemployment. Where there is neither government nor union interference with the costs of labor, there can only be voluntary unemployment. The free market offers jobs to all eager to work.

An administration that is genuinely interested in the well-being of the unemployed workers would aim at reducing the costs to business of employing them. In order to give new hope to our youth and promote on-the-job training and learning, a humanitarian administration would repeal the minimum wage legislation. Or, as a beginning, it would exempt teenagers from its restrictions. But such a repeal would require great political courage, which has adorned no president, from FDR to JC. It is more political, and yet so cruel, to promise higher wages and more benefits, although the net result can be no other than unemployment.

The pseudo-humanitarian push for higher labor costs is reinforced by the popular drive for generous unemployment compensation and other benefits for the poor and under-privileged. While we tax and discourage labor, we subsidize unemployment with great generosity. But we are harming millions of people economically and morally: the working population that is chafing under the growing burden of transfer taxation and, above all, the idle millions who are making the collection of public benefits a primary way of life. Unskilled workers whose earnings are relatively small can easily be caught in the intricate web of unemployment benefits. Why should a laborer seek employment at $100 a week if his unemployment benefits, supplementary compensations, severance pay and union support, food stamps, etc., equal or exceed this amount?

CYCLICAN UNEMPLOYMENT

A particular brand of institutional unemployment is cyclical in nature. It swells the ranks of jobless workers during economic recessions and depressions. According to mainstream economic doctrine, this kind of unemployment results from fluctuations in the demand for investment or capital goods. Businessmen may make changes in investments which are amplified in a cumulative, multiplied fashion. They will add to the stock of capital, or make net investments only, when the level of national income is growing. Prosperity must come to an end and recession ensue when sales go down, or even when they merely level off or grow at a lower rate than previously. On the other hand, investment demand can be induced by growth of sales and incomes.

This "acceleration principle" induces Keynesian policy makers to apply a great number of measures that aim at stimulating income. Wage increases, tax reductions, and rebates for lower-income earners, together with "expansionist" monetary policies, are supposed to promote consumption, the moving force for full employment and economic growth.

The doctrine is as old as it is fallacious. It is built on the ancient myth that the stimulator and spender, i.e., government, is an entity outside and above the economic process, that it owns something that is not derived from its citizens, and that it can spend this mythical something for full employment and other purposes. Actually — we must again and again repeat this truism — the government can spend only what it takes away from taxpayers and inflation victims. Any additional spending by government curtails the citizens' spending by its full amount.

The business cycle with its phases of boom and depression is the inevitable consequence of inflation and credit expansion. When the federal government suffers a budget deficit, it may raise the needed money through borrowing the people's savings, or through the creation of new money and credit by the banking system under the direction of the Federal Reserve. To borrow and consume savings is to invite an immediate recession, for the Treasury now consumes the funds that were financing economic production. As interest rates rise business must curtail its operations. Therefore, lest all private industries contract as federal spending expands, the federal government resorts to inflation and credit expansion. Deficit financing completely muddles the situation. Even though the government is consuming more resources, and capital funds, interest rates do not rise, but actually decline — at least temporarily — because of the creation of new money. Declining interest rates now misguide businessmen who embark upon expansion and modernization projects, and mislead them to participate in an economic boom that must soon collapse for lack of genuine savings. Business costs, especially in the capital goods industries, soar until production becomes unprofitable. At this point the decline sets in. Projects are cancelled, output is curtailed, and costs are reduced. In short, the depression that is caused by a falsification of interest rates leading to structural maladjustments is alleviated through readjustment and repair of the damage inflicted by the credit expansion, i.e., through a decline in investments and employment.

The Keynesians and their practitioners in government are loudly proclaiming that they have learned to cope with the

cycle. Actually, they are not avoiding the cycles by refraining —
for the moment — from deficit spending and inflation, they are
merely "solving" the dilemma of stagnation and decline
through ever larger bursts of deficit spending and money
creation. Every administration is desperately spending and
inflating in order to kindle another boom. Then, after a while,
the boom is followed by another recession that necessitates an
even larger deficit and more inflation. Unfortunately, this
merry-go-round, which characterizes the federal administra-
tions from FDR to JC, has debilitated the dollar, and has
turned individuals' savings, which should have been channeled
into job-creating investments, into means of financing federal
deficit spending.

During the boom, capital and labor are attracted by the
feverish conditions in the capital goods industries. Here
employment tends to rise as labor moves from consumer goods
industries to the booming capital goods market. There may
even be some unemployed workers who now find jobs under
boom conditions, which may temporarily reduce the general
rate of unemployment. But the boom passes by the millions of
workers who are condemned to idleness by minimum wage
legislation, labor union policies, and the temptations of
unemployment compensation and food stamps.

When the fever finally gives way to the chills of recession,
the capital goods industries undergo a painful contraction.
Capital and labor are set free. They now return to the long-
neglected consumer goods industries whence they came. In an
unhampered labor market the readjustment would be brief
and direct. But in a market that is obstructed by 65 weeks of
generous unemployment compensation, as was the case in
1976, and many other benefits, the readjustment process must
be slow and circuitous. Unemployment rises and stays high for
long periods of time.

During the boom and bust cycles, goods prices rise as a

result of the various injections of new money by the full-employment planners. During the boom, capital goods prices increase faster than consumer goods prices. During the depression, when these retreat in contraction and readjustment, consumers goods prices rise faster, which utterly confounds the Keynesians. The phenomenon of rising unemployment together with rising consumer prices painfully contradicts the acceleration principle and completely jumbles the Phillips Curve.

HEDGE UNEMPLOYMENT

The Keynesian commitment to expansionary policies is a commitment to inflation that does not promote full employment. It does not achieve the "miracle . . . of turning a stone into bread," but generates a business cycle with periods of high unemployment. Continued application of the Keynesian recipe must finally lead to the complete breakdown of the monetary system and to mass unemployment.

Rampant inflation destroys the capital markets that sustain economic production. The lenders who sustain staggering losses from currency depreciation are unable to grant new loans to finance business. And even if some loan funds should survive the destruction, lenders shy away from long-term monetary contracts. Business capital, especially long-term loan capital, becomes very scarce, which causes economic stagnation and decline. To salvage their shrinking wealth, capitalists learn to hedge for financial survival; they invest in durable goods that are expected to remain unaffected by the inflation and depreciation. They buy real estate and objects of art, gold, silver and jewelry, rare books, coins, stamps and antique grandfather clocks. This redirection of capital promotes the industries that provide the desired hedge objects, while other industries contract. There will be more demand for real estate agents and art dealers and less demand for steel workers. As the hedge industries are capital-intensive, working with relatively little labor, and the contracting industries are rather labor-intensive with a great number of workers, the readjustment entails rising unemployment. Of course, the readjustment process is hampered by labor union rules, generous unemployment compensation, and ample food stamps.

Similarly, double-digit inflation causes businessmen to hedge for financial survival. They tend to invest their working capital in those real goods they know best, in inventory and capital equipment. Funds that were serving production for the market become fixed investments in durable goods that may escape the monetary depreciation. Economic output, especially for consumers, tends to decline, which raises goods prices and swells the unemployment rolls.

DEFICIT DEVOURS JOBS

Both federal deficits and the inflation that follows consume productive capital. The deficits of the U.S. government are consuming massive amounts of business capital that otherwise would produce economic goods, create jobs, and pay wages. During the 1950's total U.S. government deficits amounted to a mere $17.7 billion and during the 60's to only $56.9 billion. During the first half of the 1970's, deficits rose to $71.4 billion, and, as if they were following an exponential curve, in the second half of this decade, they are likely to exceed $200 billion.

Inflation itself is a powerful destroyer of productive capital. It taps the savings of many millions of thrifty individuals for government consumption and redistribution. It weakens the capital markets and misleads businessmen into costly management errors. It causes businessmen to overstate their earnings because the tax laws hamper adequate depreciation reserves; they overpay their taxes; and they consume their fictitious profits.

In the United States, government is attacking business

capital from both sides: it is pressing continuously toward higher levels of consumption through spending schemes and extensive redistribution of wealth and income and it is severely hampering economic production and capital formation through taxation and intervention. The environmental regulations alone are estimated to impose some $300 billion of cleanup costs on American industry during the 1970's. All such costs are "unproductive," meaning that the expenditures consume business capital without generating new production and income. They will never build factories, stores, offices, and other facilities of production. And above all, they will not afford employment to the jobless millions.

In a stagnant economy that no longer permits capital formation and business growth, the institutional pressures for higher labor costs are painfully felt in the form of rising unemployment. The job situation may even get worse when the net amount of productive capital begins to shrink as a result of excess consumption and declining production — that is, when the amount of capital invested per worker begins to decline and wage rates must readjust to lower levels. In such a situation, which in the judgment of some economists is already upon us, the institutional pressures for higher labor wages and benefits, to which labor has grown accustomed and believes itself to be entitled to, economically and morally, would generate even higher rates of unemployment. If at the same time, government should "stimulate" the sagging economy with easy money and credit, goods prices will soar alongside the unemployment rolls.

DISINTEGRATION UNEMPLOYMENT

The ultimate folly which government may inflict on its people is the imposition of price controls, which are actually not price but people controls. When goods prices soar because budget deficits run wild and monetary authorities aim to "stimulate," the very administration conducting such policies desperately reaches for the control brakes. But there is probably no other measure that so promptly and effectively disrupts economic production and weakens the currency, as comprehensive price controls. And no other policy causes more unemployment more rapidly than the imposition of stringent controls over prices.

Price controls instantly paralyze the labor market, hamper economic production, encourage consumption, and create shortages that invite an even more coercive system of rationing, allocations and priorities. Obviously, where a central authority dictates all things, where millions of prices and wages are replaced by a single directive, chaos and darkness sets over economic life. Our splendid exchange system with its magnificent division of labor disintegrates and gives way to a primitive command system. The disintegration is accompanied by mass unemployment.

Even without price controls, rampant inflation causes such serious disarrangement of markets and disruption of production that both economic disorders, boom and depression, occur simultaneously. Consumer goods industries tend to contract while capital goods industries that are producing the machines, equipment, and materials for business hedging, enjoy a feverish boom. But the labor market with all its institutional rigidities is unable to adjust to the rapid changes and therefore suffers the strains of rising unemployment. Moreover, the disintegration of the exchange system as a result of the failure of money, the medium of exchange, causes a general decline in real wages which breeds widespread labor unrest. Individual productivity may fall, which boosts business costs. Labor unions react with militant demands and ugly strikes, which inflict losses on business and cause even more unemployment. While millions of idle workers are searching for jobs, other millions are marching on picket lines in protest against the rampant inflation that is engulfing their jobs and livelihoods. Such are the symptoms of the destruction of a currency that started out as a Keynesian stimulant and a medium for redistribution.

The capsized Keynesian ship is sinking. The property loss is staggering, but the crew is safe. Experience, which is the best of teachers, comes at a dreadfully high price. It teaches slowly, and at the cost of mistakes. But are we listening and learning?

FOOTNOTES

1. Paul A. Samuelson: *Economics*, 10th Edition, McGraw-Hill Book Company New York, 1977 p. 820.

III

UNEMPLOYMENT AND INFLATION[1]

Henry Hazlitt

For many years it has been popularly assumed that inflation increases employment. In his famous textbook, *Economics*, Paul A. Samuelson, for instance, argued: "An increase in prices is usually associated with an increase in employment. In mild inflation the wheels of industry are well lubricated and total output goes up. Private investments are brisk, and jobs plentiful. Thus a little inflation is usually to be preferred to a little deflation."

"Mild inflation," Professor Samuelson defined in the earlier editions as "less than 5 per cent," and in the fourth edition of 1958 as "2 per cent." But even a two percent annual increase in prices means that the cost of living rises by 78 percent in thirty years, and the value of the dollar decreases correspondingly.

This "prosperity through mild inflation" theory has been the economic "wisdom" which literally millions of students have been taught all over the world for the past thirty years, and many of them now hold responsible, if not policy-making positions.

THE FALSE ASSUMPTIONS

The belief that inflation creates employment rests on naive and on more sophisticated grounds. The naive belief goes like this: When more money is printed, people have more "purchasing power;" they buy more goods, and employers take on more workers to increase their total production.

The more sophisticated view was expounded by Irving Fisher as early as 1926: "When the dollar is losing value, or in other words when the price level is rising, a businessman finds his receipts rising as fast, on the average, as this general rise in prices, but not his expenses, because his expenses consist, to a large extent, of things which are contractually fixed .... Employment is then stimulated ... for a time at least." [2]

Fisher thus assumed that prices — and employment — would tend to rise faster than costs, including wages, which seemed to make sense on basis of the experiences of the 1920's.

Thirty years later, however, the British economist A. W. Phillips came up with a different observation. In an article, published in 1958,[3] he showed that over the preceding century employment apparently rose when money wage-rates rose, and vice versa.

This, too, seemed a plausible relationship. Given a period for the most part noninflationary, but in which capital investment and invention were raising the unit-productivity of labor, profit margins on employment would be rising, in some years much more than in others; and in these years the demand for labor would increase, and employers would bid up wage-rates. The increased demand for labor would lead both to higher wages and to increased employment. Phillips may have seen what he thought he saw.

There are thus two seemingly contradictory theories, yet both of them appear plausible. Fisher thought that over-all employment would increase if prices rose faster than wages, and this view was still defended by Keynes in the 1930's. In the 1950's, on the other hand, Phillips argued that on basis of past experience employment rose as wages increased.

THE APPLICATION OF THE PHILLIPS CURVE

Struck by the Phillips thesis, and seeing in it a confirmation of their own belief, the post-Keynesians of the 1960's and 1970's began to construct Phillips Curves of their own, based not on a comparison of wage-rates and employment, but on general prices and employment. And they announced that they had found that there was a "trade-off" between unemployment and prices. Price stability and reasonably full employment, they asserted, just cannot exist at the same time. The more we get of the one the less we can have of the other. We must make a choice. If we choose a low level of inflation, or none at all, we have to reconcile ourselves to a high level of unemployment. If we choose a low level of unemployment, we must reconcile ourselves to a high rate of inflation.

This alleged dilemma has served as a rationalization for continued inflation in many countries when every other excuse has run out.

THE PHILLIPS CURVE AND THE FACTS

Actually, the Phillips Curve, as interpreted by the post-Keynesians, is a myth, and in the last few years it has been increasingly recognized as a myth. At the end of this chapter there appears a table comparing the percent changes in the Consumer Price Index for the thirty years from 1948 to 1977 inclusive, with the percent rate of unemployment in the same years.

The average annual price rise in the thirty years was 3.4 percent, and the average unemployment rate 5.1 percent. If the alleged Phillips Curve relationship held dependably, then in any year in which the price rise (the "inflation" rate) went above 3.4 percent the unemployment rate should fall below 5.1 percent. Conversely, in any year in which the "inflation" rate fell below 3.4 percent, the unemployment rate would rise above 5.1 percent. This relationship would hold for all the thirty years. If, on the other hand, the Phillips Curve were inoperative or nonexistent, the probabilities are that the relationship would hold only half the time. This is exactly what we find. Fifteen out of thirty years, prices and the rate of employment acted as they should according to the Phillips Curve, and the other fifteen years they acted the other way.

A more detailed analysis of the table hardly helps. An economist who saw what had happened between 1948 and 1964 might have been excused for being impressed with the Phillips Curve, for its posited relationship held in 13 of the 17 years. But an economist who saw only what happened in the last 13 of those 30 years — from 1965 to 1977 — might have been equally excused for suspecting that the real relationship was the exact opposite of what the Phillips Curve assumed, for in that period it was borne out in only two years and proven wrong in eleven.

And even the economists who only studied what happened between 1948 and 1964 would have noted some strange anomalies. In 1951, when the Consumer Price Index rose 7.9 percent, unemployment was 3.3 percent; in 1952, when prices rose only 2.2 percent unemployment fell to 3.0 percent; and in 1953, when prices rose 8/10 of 1 percent, unemployment fell further to 2.9 percent.

Phillips statisticians can play with these figures in various ways, to see whether they can extract any more convincing correlations. They can try, for example, to find whether the

Phillips Curve relationship holds any better if the rise in the Consumer Price Index is measured from December to December, or if the calculations are remade to allow for a lag of three months, or six months, or a year, between the "inflation" rate and the unemployment rate. But they won't have any better luck. If the reader will make the count allowing for one year's lag between the price rise and the unemployment figure, for example, he will find that the Phillips Curve contention is borne out in only ten and contradicted in the other twenty years.

A clearer picture of the relationship — or nonrelationship — of price rises and unemployment emerges if we take only the last 15 years of the thirty-year period, and make our comparisons for the average of five year periods:

PRICE CHANGES AND CHANGES IN UNEMPLOYMENT[4]

	Average Annual Rise in Consumer Price Index	Average Rate of Unemployment
1961-1965	1.3%	5.5%
1966-1970	4.3%	3.9%
1971-1975	6.8%	6.1%

The highest rate of inflation during the 15 year period was accompanied by the highest rate of unemployment. And this is even more obviously the case for 1976 and 1977, when prices rose by 5.8 and 6.5 points respectively, or about 80 percent faster than the 30-year average, while unemployment stood at 7.7 percent and 7.0 percent, or about 45 percent above the average.

EXPERIENCES ABROAD

The experience of other nations has been even more striking. In August 1975 the Conference Board published a study comparing the percentages of the work forces *employed* with consumer price indices in seven industrial nations over the preceding 15 years. By this measurement, the relationship did not noticeably belie the Phillips Curve in the United States, Canada and Sweden.[5] In the four other countries in the Conference Board study the relation of employment and inflation was emphatically the opposite of that assumed by the Phillips Curve.

The steady price rise in Germany from 1967 to 1973 was accompanied by an equally steady fall in the rate of employment. In Japan a rise of 19 percent in consumer prices in 1973 and of 21 percent in 1974 was accompanied by a fall in employment. In Italy, though consumer prices began to soar in 1968, reaching a 25 percent annual rate in 1974, employment declined during the period. In some says the record of Great Britain, where the Phillips Curve was invented, was the worst of all. Though consumer prices soared 18 percent in 1974 from a rate of 4 percent a decade earlier, employment actually declined. And in 1975, a year not included in the Conference Board compilation, the British Consumer Price Index rose 24 percent and employment fell further.

But informed economists, with memories, did not need to wait for the experience of the 1970's to develop a distrust in the relationship posited by the Phillips Curve. Unemployment was high during the years of rising inflation in Germany after the first World War, and it skyrocketed during the last months of run-away inflation. Unemployment in the trade unions was 6.3 percent in August, 1923; 9.9 percent in September; 19.1 percent in October; and 23.4 percent in November when the new Rentenmark was created on basis of one trillion old marks for one new Rentenmark. The chaotic conditions created by the run-away inflation could not be remedied over-night, and in December 1923, unemployment reached the all-time peak of 28.2 percent, from which it declined sharply in 1924 as the economy and the public gained confidence in the new Mark.

THE FALLACIES OF THE
PHILLIPS CURVE THEORY

There is a whole nest of fallacies wrapped in the Phillips Curve, but the most glaring of them is the implication that the absence of inflation is the sole, or at least the chief, cause of unemployment. There can be scores of causes. One is tempted to say that there can be as many distinguishable causes for unemployment as there are unemployed. But even if we look only at the unemployment brought about by governmental policies, we can find at least a dozen different types of measures that achieve this: minimum-wage laws; regulations and laws granting special privileges and immunities to labor unions and imposing special compulsions on employers to make concessions (in the U.S., for instance, the Norris-LaGuardia Act of 1932, the Wagner Act of 1935, and the literally tens of thousands of rules and regulations imposed by the Department of Labor and labor courts); unemployment insurance; direct relief; food stamps; and so on. Whenever powerful unions are given the additional power to impose their demands not only through strike threats, strikes and intimidation, but also by special laws and regulations imposed on employers by the government, the unions almost invariably demand and obtain above-market wage increases which raise the rate of unemployment. This explains in part at least the declining ability of American industry to compete in world markets, not only with regard to consumer goods, such as textiles and shoes, but also to basic production goods including steel, machinery and ship-building.

And as the rate of chronic unemployment rises, unemployment insurance becomes increasingly generous and is paid for longer and longer periods. A study prepared by the U.S. Department of Labor in February, 1975 finally conceded that "the more liberal the unemployment insurance benefits, the higher the unemployment rate will be."

As long ago as 1934, in the early days of the New Deal, the well-known economist Benjamin M. Anderson remarked: "We can have just as much unemployment as we want to pay for." And the government is buying today a huge amount of unemployment!

Yet when the monthly unemployment figures are published, the overwhelming majority of commentators and politicians forget all about this, and instead attribute the high unemployment figure to insufficient federal spending, insufficient deficits, insufficient inflation.

Another thing wrong with the Phillips Curve is the blind trust which its advocates place in the official unemployment statistics. "Full Employment" does not mean that "everybody has a job," but merely that everybody in the "labor force" has a job — or at least 96 or 97 percent of the "labor force." And there is considerable disagreement as to what constitutes "the labor force." Out of a total population in 1978 of about 218 million, about 100 million, or 46 percent, were estimated to be part of the "civilian labor force." In 1975, just three years earlier, the percentage was about 43 percent, a relative increase in the "labor force" by about three million workers!

As only 91,346,000 persons were estimated as being employed as of June, 1978, this left about 5.7 million "unemployed."

But nobody ever actually counted the "unemployed," and all the figures shown here are estimates, subject to various degrees of error. In fact there is actually no way ever to count the unemployed or make "objective" estimates, because the basic notions of what constitutes "labor force" and who should be regarded as "unemployed" involve strong subjective elements.

As the British economist A. C. Pigou wrote some forty years ago; "A man is only unemployed when he is *both* not employed and *also* desires to be employed." It is this second requirement which we can never measure. When men and women are being paid enough unemployment insurance on relief or food stamps to feel no great urgency to take a job, the raw government statistics can give a very misleading impression of the hardships of unemployment.

INFLATION AND PUBLIC ATTITUDES

When we put aside all questions of exact quantitative determination and alleged Phillips Curves, it is nonetheless clear that inflation does affect employment in numerous ways.

At its beginning, inflation can tend to create more employment, for the reason that Irving Fisher gave a long time ago: Inflation tends to increase sales and selling prices faster than it increases costs. But this effect is only temporary, and occurs only to the extent that the inflation is unexpected. For in a short time costs catch up with retail selling prices. To prevent this the inflation must be continued. But as soon as people *expect* the inflation to continue, they will make compensating adjustments and demands. Unions ask for higher wage-rates and "escalating" clauses, lenders demand higher interest rates, including "price premiums," and so on. To keep stimulating employment, it is not enough for the government to continue inflating at the old rate, however high; it must accelerate the inflation. But as soon as people *expect even the acceleration,* this too becomes futile for providing more employment.

Meanwhile, even if the inflation is relatively mild — only "2 percent" as suggested by Professor Samuelson — and proceeds at a fairly even rate, it begins to create distortions in the economy. It is amazing how systematically this is overlooked. Most journalists, and even most economists, make the tacit assumption that an inflation increases prices *uniformly* — that if the wholesale or consumers price index has gone up about 10 percent in a year, all prices have gone up about 10 percent. This assumption is seldom made consciously and explicitly; if it were it would be more often detected and refuted.

The assumption is never correct. Even apart from the wide differences in the elasticity of demand for different commodities, the new money that the government prints and pays out in an inflation does not go proportionately or simultaneously to everybody. It goes, say, to government contractors and their employees, and these first receivers spend it on the particular goods and services they want. The producers of these goods, and their employees, in turn spend the money for still other goods and services. And so on. The first groups spend the money when prices have gone up least; the final groups when prices have gone up most. In addition, the growing realization that inflation will continue, itself changes the direction of demand — away from thrift and toward luxury spending, for example.

Thus while inflation is going on it always brings about a misdirection of production and employment. It leads to a condition of temporary demand for various goods, and hence increased employment in specific sectors, while in other sectors of the economy unemployment increases. At the end of every inflation there is certain to be a so-called stabilization crisis," as the misallocation of resources comes to an end.

But even the distorted and misdirected employment cannot be indefinitely maintained by continuing or accelerating the inflation. For inflation, as it goes, on, more and more distorts *relative* prices and *relative* wages, and disrupts workable relations between particular prices and particular wage-rates. While some producers confront swollen and unmeetable demand, others are being driven out of business as wages and other costs rise faster than their own selling prices. And as inflation accelerates it becomes impossible for individual producers to make any dependable estimate of the wage rates and other costs they will have to meet in the next few months, or their own future selling price, or the margin between the two. The result is not only increasing malemployment, but increasing unemployment.

Nor can the government mitigate the situation by any such further intervention as "indexing." If it tries to insure, for example, that all workers are paid the average increase that has occurred in wages and prices, it will not only increase wages over the previous average, but put out of business even sooner the producers who have not been able, because of lack of demand, to raise their selling prices as much as the average. Every attempt to correct previous distortions and inequities by government ukase will only create worse distortions and inequities.

There is no cure but to halt the inflation. But the process of stabilizing the currency is in itself not without cost. There is likely to be at least a temporary increase in unemployment, and there may be a slowing down in the rate of economic growth. But that cost is infinitely less than that of continuing the inflation — or even of trying to slow it down "gradually."

In sum, inflation can increase employment only temporarily, only to the extent that it is unexpected, and only when it is comparatively mild and in its early stages. This was the period of the "fool's paradise" of the 1960's. On the other hand, the long-run effect of inflation, as millions of Americans have come to realize during the 1970's, must be to misdirect employment and finally to disorganize the economy.

The belief that inflation reduces unemployment is perhaps the most costly myth of the present age.

PERCENT CHANGE

Year	CPI	Percent Unemployment
1948	7.8	3.8
1949	-1.0	5.9
1950	1.0	5.3
1951	7.9	3.3
1952	2.2	3.0
1953	.8	2.9
1954	.5	5.5
1955	-.4	4.4
1956	1.5	4.1
1957	3.6	4.3
1958	2.7	6.8
1959	.8	5.5
1960	1.6	5.5
1961	1.0	6.7
1962	1.1	5.5
1963	1.2	5.7
1964	1.3	5.2
1965	1.7	4.5
1966	2.9	3.8
1967	2.9	3.8
1968	4.2	3.6
1969	5.4	3.5

1970	5.9	4.9
1971	4.3	5.9
1972	3.3	5.6
1973	6.2	4.9
1974	11.0	5.6
1975	9.1	8.5
1976	5.8	7.7
1977	6.5	7.0

Source: Economic Report of the President
January, 1978, pp. 318 and 291.

FOOTNOTES

1. Much of the material in this chapter is taken from Chapter 14 of the author's *The Inflation Crisis And How to Resolve It*, Copyright 1978 by Henry Hazlitt. Reprinted by permission of the publishers, Arlington House, New Rochelle, N.Y.
2. "A Statistical Relation between Unemployment and Price Changes." *International Labor Review*, June 1926, pp. 785-792.
3. "The Relation between Unemployment and the Rate of Change of Money Wage Rates in the United Kingdom, 1861-1957," *Economica*, November, 1958, pp. 283-299.
4. The table was suggested by one which appeared in Milton Friedman's *Newsweek* column of Dec. 6. 1976.
5. In our thirty years table for the United States, however, we saw that when the price increase figure shot up in 1974 to 11 percent from 6.2 percent in 1973, unemployment also rose. If we look at 1975 — not shown in the Conference Board study — we find that unemployment soared to 8.5 percent even though prices rose by 9.1 percent. And in 1976 and 1977 the price-employment ratio belied the Phillips Curve even more strikingly. Similarly, if we consider what happened in 1975 in Canada, we find that though consumer prices rose by the unusually high rate of 10.7 percent, the index of manufacturing employment in Canada fell from 108.9 in 1974 to 102.8 in 1975.

IV

THE LABOR UNION MONOPOLY

Reed Larson

Some twenty years ago, in the 1950's, when unemployment rarely reached four percent and the rate of inflation averaged less than two percent a year, Donald Richberg bluntly warned that the concentration of power in the hands of "under-regulated, under-criticized, under-investigated, tax-exempt, and specially privileged labor organizations — and in their belligerent, aggressive, and far-too-often lawless and corrupt managers" has changed the union movement so that "instead of being a movement of workers banded together for the protection and advancement of their legitimate interests in a free economy, the labor movement has now become a political movement with the objective of establishing a socialist labor government in control of the economic and social life of the nation."[1]

Richberg was not an enemy of labor. In fact, in the 1920's he acted as the chief counsel of railway unions in their fight against the government, and he won a reputation by defending unions against corporations. He helped to draft the Railway Labor Act passed by Congress in 1926, and in the early years of the New Deal drafted the labor provisions of the National Industrial Recovery Act which created the NRA. But the developments which he observed between the early days of the New Deal and the 1950's changed his mind; especially the growing trend of forcing workers to join unions.

Through the widespread practice of compulsory unionism, millions of Americans are compelled to support political and ideological positions with which they may not agree, and which many believe are not in the public interest. Most Americans agree, of course, that a union, a union member as an individual, or anyone else, should have the right to peacefully advocate any economic theory whatsoever. But this does not mean that an individual worker should be forced to support, and help to finance, policies with which he does not agree at the risk of losing his job. Nevertheless, this is exactly what is happening today, and worse yet, government-sanctioned union coercion is a major factor in establishing public policies which undermine the vitality of the American economic system, and thereby contribute to the problem of unemployment — which hurts all workers, including union members.

THE ORIGIN OF UNION POWER

Labor union monopoly is primarily a product of government action. The process began in 1926 with the Railway Labor Act, which was co-authored by the same Donald Richberg who at that time was a union lawyer. The pattern continued through the Norris-LaGuardia Act and culminated in 1935 in the passage of the Wagner Act, known officially as the National Labor Relations Act.

The NLRA is based on the premise that it is in the public interest to herd employees into collective groups rather than to deal with them as individuals. It was not intended to be evenhanded. It was designed to be pro-union. The law denies men and women the right to represent themselves if they wish, and puts the stamp of governmental approval on a system which compels employees to pay a labor union for the right to earn a living. This labor policy subordinates the rights of individual employees — and employers — to the privileges and powers of union organizers.

The essential features of the 1935 policy remain unchanged to this day. It is not widely understood that the Taft-Hartley Act did not change the basic policy of the Wagner Act. Taft-Hartley merely treated some of the symptoms of union monopoly power — mostly through greater government intervention in labor-management relations. The 1959 Landrum-Griffin Act was more of the same medicine — this time an effort by government to regulate the internal affairs of unions in an attempt to control abuses growing out of earlier grants of special privilege to labor union organizers.

Recognition of these basic weaknesses in our monopoly-producing national labor policy has come from numerous authorities, occupying all points in the philosophical spectrum. Sylvester Petro, in his characteristically straightforward manner, denounces the "collectivist principles animating the NLRA," labeling them "anti-libertarian" and "economically destructive." According to Texas University Professor George Schatzki, himself a former union lawyer and ACLU activist, "individual interests have received short shrift under the National Labor Relations Act in a variety of contexts." A few years ago Dean Roscoe Pound concluded that "the labor leader and labor union now stand where king and government and landowner and charity and husband and father stood at common law." Even Archibald Cox has denounced the legal curtailment of worker rights, declaring that "there are many ways, legal as well as illegal, by which entrenched [union] officials can 'take care of' recalcitrant members."[2] The statement appeared originally in 1960 in the Michigan Law Review," and Professor Cox has never retracted it, yet he has made it quite clear in the meantime that he does not propose to protect the American working people by giving them the choice of joining or not joining a union. Writing on American labor law, the 1974 Nobel Prize winner, Professor F. A. von Hayek, sums it up in these words: "They [The labor unions] have become the only important instance in which governments signally fail in their prime function — the prevention of coercion and violence . . . It cannot be stressed enough that the coercion which unions have been permitted to exercise contrary to all principles of freedom under the law is primarily the coercion of fellow workers."[3] The Hayek statement, like several of the others, was written more than fifteen years ago. However, there has been no important change in federal labor policy since that time, which in itself is something of a victory for the union hierarchy. All the major battles over labor legislation in recent years have been against measures to enlarge even further the powers and privileges of union officials, not to curtail them.

Just what kind of an organization has grown out of more than forty years of government-sanctioned monopoly and special privilege? The union movement today is a political and economic giant collecting an estimated $2 billion a year in forced dues from workers who would be fired from their jobs if they refused to pay; it is a nationwide network staffed by tens of thousands of officers and employees whose total payroll is conservatively estimated at $1 billion a year; it is an organization which, in the words of its own spokesmen, places political action at the top of its priority list, and which uses a substantial part of its vast resources directly for political action.[4]

THE UNIONS AND UNEMPLOYMENT

Given this vast power, one might expect that the unions and their officials would have primarily asserted themselves on behalf of their members — forced or otherwise — and in particular that they would have devoted their power to solving what George Meany has termed "the human recession of unemployment." Such is the conventional wisdom. After all, did not the AFL-CIO state repeatedly throughout the 1976 political campaign that unemployment was "the single most important issue" facing the country?[5] Did not Meany in his 1976 Labor Day speech declare that "solving the unemployment problem is the key to the problem of poverty, adequate housing, decent medical care and civil rights?"[6] And did not the AFL-CIO Executive Council in February 1977 officially list a public jobs program among the Federation's highest priorities?[7]

The answer to these questions is, of course, yes. Yes, the union leadership makes a great deal of noise about unemployment. But behind the rhetoric, the harsh facts suggest that the monopoly power of the unions has actually contributed to unemployment. In fact, union monopoly power, if we consider both its direct and indirect results, may very well be the single greatest factor in creating unemployment. This occurs in two ways: first, as a direct result of uneconomic wage settlements, and second, indirectly, through the use of its political power.

EXCESSIVE WAGE DEMANDS

When union power is so great that it can extract from an employer — or, more significantly, from an entire industry — wage rates which are higher than the free market will sustain, unemployment can — and generally does — result. Unemployment results first because, as Professor Hayek argues, the union contract will make it uneconomical to employ workers whose productivity is below the wage rate, and second, because excessively high wages, if passed along in higher prices, will result in a lowering of demand and, consequently, of employment.[8]

A case in point is the 1976 UAW contract which secured an extra twelve days paid vacation per year for auto workers. The purpose, according to union spokesmen, is to "make work" by forcing the auto industry to hire more workers than they would otherwise do. Ironically, the contract seems to have had precisely the opposite result.

According to a 1977 study by the Council on Wage and Price Stability, if the increase in labor costs is not offset by a corresponding increase in productivity, two unwanted results will ensue: demand for American cars will fall and the auto industry will be forced to use more labor-saving machinery. The end result may be "fewer jobs for U.S. auto workers."[9]

Interestingly, the unexpurgated version of this report was not intended for publication. But, unfortunately for the future of the Council on Wage and Price Stability, the report was leaked to the press before it could go through the watering down process dictated by political considerations.

Not surprisingly, the AFL-CIO promptly termed the Council a "dismal failure" and called for its abolition.[10]

The UAW settlement, of course, is unusual only because of its specific provisions. The results — caused by an uneconomic rise in wages and/or benefits — are typical of many union-forced agreements.

And at least some of those workers who are made unemployable because of artificially high wage levels resulting from union economic power are loaded onto the back of the taxpayers through the use of union political power. Union strategy places heavy emphasis on the broadening of various forms of government dole and the creation of tax-funded, make-work programs for the unemployed, some of whom are in that condition precisely because of union action.

THE UNIONS' POLITICAL POWER

This brings us to the second area through which the union monopoly contributes to unemployment — the use of political power to establish legislative policies which can only add further to the ranks of the unemployed. This aspect is less widely recognized, but is actually far more damaging to the public interest in its ultimate impact.

Again, it is important to note the incredible size of the union political machinery. Too often observers of the political scene have their attention riveted on the "hard money" which unions collect and turn over to political candidates. This "hard money" — the cash political contributions — usually adds up to only a paltry $10 or $15 million in a federal election year. Of far greater importance is the hidden and unreported union political spending — the use of much of their $90-million-a-month staff network, with all its supporting organizational costs, primarily for political work for months preceding a federal election.

Labor columnist Victor Riesel estimates the biennial cost of union political spending to be in excess of $100 million — a figure which surpasses the combined totals spent in 1976 by the two major political parties, even when adding the nearly $50 million extracted from the taxpayers to finance presidential campaigns.[11]

It's important to emphasize that there are absolutely no solid figures on which to base this estimate. There are no published data and we can only make a projection based on various bits and pieces which give a picture of the magnitude of the actual union political effort. Douglas Caddy in his famous book, *The One Hundred Million Dollar Payoff*, suggested that figure.[12] Victor Riesel says it is more than a hundred million; and in view of the emphasis on politics by union leaders, and the fact that the unions take in and spend about $4 billion a year, total political spending of $100 million would be only 2½ percent of total union spending, which seems definitely on the low side.

This massive union political machine, moreover, is dedicated almost exclusively to candidates, issues, and causes which reduce incentive and discourage capital formation. Consider, for example, the positions taken by the AFL-CIO on various issues during the 94th Congress.[13]

They lobbied for, among other things, national economic "planning;" an increased federal budget and more deficit spending; increased federal jobs programs; and removal of tax incentives for businesses and individuals. They are strong backers of the array of business-harassing regulatory schemes which are smothering small businessmen across America with a blizzard of federal paperwork. Few, if any, of those proposals would ever have become law without the very substantial support of the officials of organized labor.

Many observers say that union political influence is neutral on the "free market versus collectivist" scale, that there are "conservative" unions and "liberal" unions, and that their activities tend to balance each other out insofar as economic issues are concerned.

To test this thesis, the National Right-to-Work Committee undertook an analysis of the legislative program during the 94th Congress of the supposedly "conservative" branch of the union movement — the AFL-CIO. The results: if the AFL-CIO had been a Congressman, it would have scored 100 percent on liberal ADA index, an impressive feat achieved only by the most devoted of the faithful. And most people will agree that the program of the Americans for Democratic Action is not one that enhances the free market system or encourages the creation of employment in the private sector of business.

On twenty-three key issues, Mr. Meany's AFL-CIO and Congresswoman Bella Abzug took the same position 95 percent of the time, which would apparently give the unions a 95 percent score on the "Bella Abzug index." Furthermore, by their own definition, the AFL-CIO was concerned with "labor legislation" only twenty percent of the time. Eighty percent of their legislative program dealt with issues unrelated, or only peripherally related, to the area of labor-management relations. And that is the record of the so-called "conservative" wing of the union movement. The "liberal" wing of unionism is a substantial political force in its own right and growing in its influence every day.

IMPACT OF UNION POLICIES ON EMPLOYMENT

Even though unions deny the fact, many of the political programs which they support tend to impede employment and hence make for increased unemployment. Under intense union pressure, Congress in 1977 passed, by a 236 to 187 vote, a new minimum wage bill which provided for an increase in the Federal minimum wage from $2.30 an hour to $2.65, as of January 1, 1978, up to $2.90 in 1979, $3.10 in 1980, and $3.35 in 1981, a more than 45 percent increase in four years. In signing the bill, President Carter admitted that while "the overall effect will be good," higher minimum wages will cause more unemployment among those who are least employable, teenagers and especially black youth. Study after study by reputable observers, including government agencies,[14] has established the critical role played by minimum wages in discouraging employment of marginal workers. And yet the union leaders, apparently blind to the evidence, pressured Congress into voting the unprecedented increase in minimum

wages which added an estimated $2 billion to the wage cost in
the first year alone, thus raising the cost of living in general
and denying many of the young and unskilled a chance to earn
a living and, at the same time, gain needed experience and
training.[15]

UNEMPLOYMENT IN THE CONSTRUCTION INDUSTRIES

It's the same story with regard to the Davis-Bacon Act,
which requires that on all construction jobs involving federal
funds "prevailing wages" must be paid, i.e., in effect the
maximum union wages, even if large numbers of workers are
unemployed who would be willing to work for less. During the
94th Congress the AFL-CIO supported attempts to expand the
application of the Act's "fair wage requirements" to cover the
federal revenue sharing program.[16] The proposal was defeated
in the House. But the fact remains that Davis-Bacon requirements increase construction costs — perhaps, as Senator Orrin
Hatch claimed, by as much as 5-15 percent or $1.5 billion a
year.[17] Professor Yale Brozen has described the Davis-Bacon
Act as "the most important single cause of high construction
costs," the principal results of which are less construction for
the federal dollar, and fewer jobs.[18]

Between 1970 and 1976 the construction industry
experienced double-digit unemployment in every year except
1973, a much higher rate of unemployment than in most
segments of the economy: and as Professor Brozen pointed out,
this was not because of a lack of potential demand, "but
because of the overpricing of construction labor."[19]

For those construction workers fortunate enough to land
a job, earnings were very good. Construction wages in 1976
were 48% higher than were wages in manufacturing.[20] In the
decade 1966-1976, according to a study by the Contractors

Mutual Association, "wages and benefits of union building trades workers rose 125 percent," while the Consumer Price Index increased by only 75 percent.[21]

However, even the array of special powers extended to all labor unions under law coupled with a number of unique added privileges enjoyed only by construction unions, has not kept the pressure of the free market from working its will. Market pressures are beginning to correct the imbalance fostered by the construction union labor monopoly.

In the face of great odds and legal disadvantages, construction by contractors who do not force their employees to join unions has experienced a phenomenal growth in the last few years, with recent statistics showing that more than 50 percent of construction is now performed by non-union craftsmen.[22] This led the building trades unions in 1975 to mount an all-out drive to pass a common situs picketing bill. Had public pressure not forced President Ford to veto the bill, expanded picketing rights would have allowed union agents to force non-union construction workers to either join the union or get off the job-site.

The campaign for this bill provided an excellent illustration of the unions' political influence bought with its tens of millions of dollars expenditure in political campaign support.

The common situs picketing bill is manifestly unpopular with the American People. It literally has no support from the general press. It has been roundly denounced editorially by newspapers ranging from *The New York Times* to *The Chicago Tribune*.[23]   An Opinion Research Corporation poll in March 1976 showed that the American people, including a heavy majority of union members, opposed the situs picketing bill by a margin of 73 to 16.[24] Still, that bill sailed through the House of Representatives by a wide margin and was passed by the Senate in a classic demonstration of union political power.

The public interest be damned: President Ford's last-minute decision to veto the bill was the only thing that prevented it from becoming law.

The unions tried again, early in 1977, obviously hoping to collect on their political IOUs before public opposition could be sufficiently aroused to register with the heavily union-obligated majorities in both houses. But this time, the House defeated the common situs picketing bill by a narrow margin of 217 to 205, apparently aware of the fact that public opposition to the bill had risen substantially since the time when President Ford first vetoed the bill in 1976. According to a Roper poll, public opinion was 77 to 12 against the bill.[25]

Even though the bill was finally defeated in 1977, this situation reveals the strength of the unions' political muscle, a force which comes down consistently on the side of measures that weaken incentive, discourage the creation of capital, jack up the minimum wage rates, and engage in assorted anti-free-market mischief, all of which tends to generate more unemployment. If it were not for the mighty political power of this government-sanctioned monopoly, the legislative climate would be radically changed for the better insofar as measures affecting the health and vitality of the economy and its job-creating capability are concerned.

THE UNION POWER BLOC

The problem is that government-granted powers have created a giant political power bloc manipulated by a handful of union officials, and as the record shows only too clearly, the policies advocated by those who control this power bloc seem always to be arrayed on the side of more government regulation, and to place more obstacles in the path of the risk-taking entrepreneur whose efforts are essential to a healthy, expanding economy.

It is possible, of course, that many — or even most — union members agree with Bella Abzug's position 95% of the time — or with the ADA position 100% of the time. It is possible but not likely.

Just as in the case of common situs picketing, the interests and aspirations of those who control the union movement are different from the interests and aspirations of the average union member. As the 1977 Roper Poll showed, union members opposed common situs picketing by a ratio of 64 to 30, while the union hierarchy was committing its entire resources to forcing the bill through Congress with the greatest possible speed. One top AFL-CIO official told *Business Week:* "We're not going to give Congress a choice. We're going to take people to the wall."[26]   The Roper Poll also showed that union members opposed compulsory unionism by a ratio of 49 to 45. Still, top union officials are devoting the full weight of their organization to forcing through Congress legislation striking down state Right-to-Work laws.

The most frightening aspect of this situation is that the United States may have reached the point where union political power can veto any effective measure to restore individual freedom and political balance. Something which might be called the ratchet effect is operating in Congress, meaning that legislation affecting union power and privilege can move in only one direction: toward greater union power, never toward less. This is well illustrated by the so-called Federal Election Reform Act of 1971 (amended in 1974 and again in 1976). Political considerations dictated that it had to be favorable to union officials. In effect, the Act curtailed the political impact of most groups, while leaving untouched the use of union money and manpower as "in-kind" political campaign support. If the bill had dealt even-handedly with union political power, it could never have been enacted by Congress.

The result, as summarized in a report appearing in the *Washington Post* of March 18, 1977 is that "the presidential campaign financing law, which barred private contributions to the major party candidates in last year's election, vastly increased the vote-getting power of organized labor ... The magnitude and sophistication of [organized] labor's efforts last year are even more impressive when stacked up against what others could do."[27] The same phenomenon can be observed in a variety of so-called reform measures in which union political power dictates that Congress must grant additional advantage and privilege to union officials in order to pass a measure.

The really crucial question, however, is not whether the union hierarchy is on one side or the other of any economic issue — even though they are usually supporting those measures which make for more unemployment — but whether unions should be permitted to use funds forced from workers as a condition of employment to promote political or ideological causes; and they are doing just that on a massive scale.

The root of that damaging power, as Professor Hayek says, is the union's ability to legally coerce fellow workers. Removal of that coercive power from union officials would have a very direct and beneficial bearing on many of the economic issues which face the nation, especially the problem of chronic unemployment.

FOOTNOTES

1. Donald R. Richberg, *Labor Union Monopoly: A Clear and Present Danger* (Chicago: Henry Regnery Company, 1957), pp. vi and vii.
2. Sylvester Petro, "Civil Liberty, Syndicalism, and the NLRA," *The University of Toledo Law Review*, Vol. 5, Number 3, Spring, 1974; pp. 448 and 449. George Schatzki, "Majority Rule, Exclusive Representation, and the Interest of Individual Workers: Should Exclusivity be Abol-

ished?" *University of Pennsylvania Law Review*, Vol. 123, Number 4, April, 1975; p. 898. Roscoe Pound, Edward H. Chamberlin, Philip D. Bradley, Gerard D. Reilly, *Labor Unions and Public Policy*, Mr. Pound wrote section IV, "Legal Immunities of Labor Unions," from which this quote comes. (Washington, D.C.: American Enterprise Association, 1958), p. 145. Archibald Cox, "Internal Affairs of Labor Unions Under the Labor Reform Act of 1959," *Michigan Law Review*, Volume 58, April, 1960; p. 853.

3. Friedrich A. Hayek, *The Constitution of Liberty* (Chicago: University of Chicago Press, 1960), pp. 267 and 269.

4. The staff's payroll figures are derived from the only public information available — a 1959 compilation of union financial reports by the Department of Labor. At that time a partial compilation — based on reports from 80% of union organizations — showed a staff payroll totaling $410,000,000, dues income of $923,000,000. A projection of this figure to a 100% sample in 1959 and normal inflation and growth for over eighteen years, places present dues income figures at well over $2 billion, staff payroll at least $1 billion, and additional union income from investments and other enterprises, at an undetermined total estimated anywhere from $1.5 to $3 billion. Labor Department reports show that about 84% of union contracts include "union security" provisions meaning some form of compulsory unionism.

5. See, for instance, George Meany, Labor Day Speech, September 5, 1976.

6. *Ibid.*

7. See statement of AFL-CIO Executive Council, February 24, 1977.

8. Hayek, *op. cit.*, chapter 18. See also Patrick M. Boarman, *Union Monopolies and Antitrust Restraints* (Washington, D.C.: Labor Policy Associates, 1963), Chapter III, "Labor Union Monopoly and Unemployment."

9. William Lilley, III, Acting Director, The Council on Wage and Price Stability, analysis of the collective bargaining agreement between the United Auto Workers and General Motors, Ford and Chrysler, January 13, 1977.

10. Statement of AFL-CIO Executive Council, February 24, 1977.

11. Victor Riesel, "Unions Collect Huge Bankroll for Campaign," *The Commercial Appeal*, [Memphis], September 5, 1976, section C, page 6.

12. Douglas Caddy, *The Hundred Million Dollar Payoff* (New Rochelle, New York: Arlington House, 1974).

13. Labor Looks at the 94th Congress: *An AFL-CIO Legislative Report* (Washington, D.C.: AFL-CIO Department of Legislation, January, 1977), p. 73.

14. The relationship of the minimum wage and unemployment has been

succinctly discussed along with the role of government in the creation of union monopoly power in a recent publication of the U.S. Chamber of Commerce: William H. Peterson, *Who is the Real Employer — The Real Source of Jobs* (Washington, D.C., 1976).

15. U.S. Department of Labor as cited in *U.S. News and World Report*, February 21, 1977, Volume LXXXII, Number 7, pp. 54 and 55.

16. "A Report on Congress — 1976," *AFL-CIO News*, September 4, 1976 Volume XXI, Number 36.

17. Senator Orrin Hatch, *Congressional Record* for January 26, 1977, p. S 1495.

18. Yale Brozen, "Measures for Improving Construction Industry Health." Paper presented before the Construction Industry Manufacturers' Association, Chicago, November 11, 1970, p. 3.

19. *Ibid.*, p. 2.

20. "Common Situs and Economic Analysis," Rinfret Associates, Inc. (New York, 1977), p. 2.

21. "Wage Gains of Union Construction Workers, January 1966-January 1976," Contractors Mutual Association (Washington, D.C., 1976), p. 4.

22. Herbert R. Northrup and Howard G. Foster, *Open Shop Construction* (Philadelphia: Industrial Research Unit, The Wharton School, University of Pennsylvania, 1975), chapter XIII.

23. See especially "Common Situs Picketing Again," *Chicago Tribune*, February 28, 1977, and "An Uncommonly Bad Bill," *New York Times*, March 12, 1977.

24. *Public Attitudes Toward Right-to-Work Laws*, a poll conducted by the Opinion Research Corporation, Princeton, New Jersey, in March, 1976. Copies of the poll are available from the National Right-to-Work Committee.

25. Poll conducted by the Roper Organization, Inc., New York, N.Y., February, 1977 as part of *Roper Reports*, #77-3.

26. "AFL-CIO: Set to Bargain Hard with Congress," *Business Week*, March 7, 1977, Number 2473, p. 68.

27. "Labor Big Victor in Vote-Getting Power," *The Washington Post*, March 18, 1977.

V

INFLATION, UNEMPLOYMENT AND "OBSCENE PROFITS"

John Q. Jennings

In his inaugural address, in January 1977, President Carter urged "faith in an old dream."

There are many "old dreams" which have been largely forgotten — to the detriment of the nation; and one of them is the old American principle of "a fair day's work for a fair day's pay." It has been replaced by the "new dream" that it is possible for individuals and nations to get something for nothing, that wages can be forced up faster than productivity without causing unemployment, inflation or both.

According to a 1973 Gallup poll, half of the workers questioned agreed that they could accomplish more every day than they did, if they only tried. And why didn't they? A 1976 Harris poll apparently gave the answer. Two-thirds of the general public and 80 percent of the hourly wage earners thought that increased productivity would merely increase the profits of the companies at the expense of the workers. Yet the same workers demand increased wages and cost of living adjustments to compensate for higher prices (which they themselves help to raise) with no regard for the need of a corresponding increase in productivity.

Some years ago it was fashionable among economists to distinguish between "demand pull" and "cost push" inflation. There is no doubt that prices will — and must — rise if the money supply increases faster than the supply of good and services. But this "monetarist" view tends to overlook the "cost push" aspect: wages rising faster than productivity, thus either pushing up prices or increasing unemployment.

The American automobile industry offers a good example of the "cost push" trend of recent years. In 1974 unit labor cost increased by 13.2 percent, in 1975 by 7.5 percent, and in 1976 by only 3.2 percent. And then came the new wage demands in early 1977. In the rubber and automobile industries the cost of wages and benefits rose by ten percent, and in the oil industry by nine percent. According to a statement by General Motors, total hourly labor cost on basis of the new contract was expected to rise by 1979, by $3.75 to a total of $15, an increase in the company's aggregate labor cost of $5.8 billion, or of about $500 per car.

Yet somehow, nobody — least of all Congress and the Administration — seemed seriously concerned about the "cost push" impact on prices and employment.

In the automobile industry the effect of the wage policies is only too obvious. In 1964, the U.S. imported virtually no cars from Japan. As one Toyota dealer described the response of the American public to Japanese cars at that time: "Man," people told him, "I wouldn't have one of them cars for nothing. I don't want to get sick." Thirteen years later, the same dealer, who couldn't "give away" a Japanese car in 1965 sold 904 Toyotas in just one month, and Japanese imports accounted for twelve percent of total car sales in the U.S.

Between 1976 and 1977 Toyota imports alone increased by

seventy percent, and foreign-made cars as a whole accounted for about twenty percent of total car sales in 1977 — while Detroit suffered from severe unemployment.

WAGES AND PRODUCTIVITY

During the 1960's, practically everybody, including most of the union leaders, agreed with President Kennedy and President Johnson that wage and benefit increases in excess of 3.2 percent, which was then regarded as the average annual rate of increase in man-hour productivity, was "inflationary." But this "old dream" of linking wage increases and productivity increases has been forgotten in recent years, which explains, at least in part, the chronic inflation, the growing unemployment, and the declining value of the dollar.

While the increase in productivity recovered to about 3.2 percent in 1977, after being well below that level for a number of years, the new wage increases of ten percent were more than three times as large as the increase in man-hour productivity. This pushed up prices and led to the closing of the least efficient units, and, hence, to more unemployment. And the situation was similar in 1978 and 1979.

Moreover, since most unions have a cost-of-living escalator clause in their contracts, they can keep up with the inflation which their own excessive wage demands helped to bring about, thereby forcing the cost of production, and prices, ever higher in a constant vicious spiral.

Clearly, not all Americans enjoy the same degree of "protection." Those who live on fixed incomes are left holding the bag — the "inflation bag." And those workers who have priced themselves out of the market become unemployed and have to be supported by those still working, thus lowering the average standard of living of all.

DETROIT AND CAR IMPORTS

Chrysler imports its "Colts" from Japan, Ford its "Fiestas" from Germany, and General Motors its "Opels" from Germany and Japan. Michigan automobile workers would be much happeir if these cars were made in Detroit, but most of them, unfortunately, refuse to face the fact that their high wages, frequent strikes, and low productivity stimulate imports and destroy American jobs. Michigan is full of Toyotas, Datsuns and Hondas which are driven by both employed and unemployed members of the UAW. Between November 1973 and May 1977 production declined by 4.8 percent in the electrical machinery industry, 6.8 percent in the textile mills, by 13.9 percent in iron and steel with a corresponding loss of jobs. By the fall of 1977, the Alan Wood Steel Company had gone out of business, Youngstown Sheet and Tube closed its Youngstown mills throwing some 5000 workers out of work, Big Steel had laid off thousands of employees throughout the country, foreign imports, especially from Japan, continued to increase. Slowly, very slowly, some of the experts began to express concern about the chronic and growing "cost push" pressure. Henry C. Wallich, a Member of the Federal Reserve Board, for instance, warned that rising wages constitute the chief cause of rising prices. As long as wages and benefits continue to increase at an average rate of eight percent or more, there is little hope of reducing inflation below six percent.

But how to convince the union leaders, the rank and file, and the politicians who are spokesmen for the unions?

THE WORKERS ARE NOT TOLD THE TRUTH

As American industries — car, steel, textiles and many others — are faced with growing competition from lower-priced imports, the companies cut production, lay off workers, and reduce investments which could produce jobs in the future. But they fail to do one thing: they do not present to their workers — or to the public in general — the "arithmetic" of the business, a simple, graphic, easily understood picture of the financial position of the company, which would enable the employees to figure out for themselves that it would be in their own interest to minimize their demands and strikes and to maximize their man-hour productivity.

The announcement of the Youngstown Sheet and Tube Company when it decided that it had to close its Youngstown facilities and lay off some 5000 workers illustrates the point. This is what R.C. Rieden, chairman of the board of Lykes Corp., the parent company of Youngstown Sheet and Tube, had to say:

> The pricing of steel products has been subjected to governmental interference by such pressures as jawboning, demands for pre-notification of price increases or rollbacks and unjustified pricing investigations, all of which have resulted in de facto price controls over the past 15 years. The steady and persistent erosion of our profit margins, strongly affected by foreign imports, governmental price restraint and mounting environmental regulation, have brought about the circumstances which required this decision.

To this Frank Leseganich, president of District 26 of the United Steelworkers Union in Youngstown replied:

> I am going to more or less put the blame on the federal government. The imports are killing us. There is no question about it . . . The imports have a strangle hold on steel producing units in this country.
>
> We have lost the shoe industry, the clothing industry, the electronic industry. I don't think there

is a typewriter made in this country. We are becoming a consumer nation, not a producer. We'll all
be out there looking for jobs fixing toasters made in
the Japanese empire.

It is, of course, very easy to blame "imports" for the plight
of many American industries. But blocking imports in order to
preserve domestic employment is hardly the solution in the
long run. It means an increase in prices for the consumer, and
hence a decline in over-all demand unless Washington creates
more fiat money which will mean still higher prices — and thus
less demand, fewer jobs and more need for additional fiat
money. Moreover, a policy of fighting imports may lead to
retaliation from the foreign countries affected. "Buy from
those who buy from us" is an old slogan, and often a very
effective one, especially in an age of nationalism. Reduced
American imports may help the workers in some industries,
but will lead almost by necessity to fewer jobs in the export
industries.

Why can Japanese steel-makers undersell American
manufacturers? It is basically not the result of illegal price
rigging, but of the materially lower production cost in Japan,
which in turn is due to three basic facts: there are far fewer
strikes and strike threats in Japan; hourly wages are lower;
and, most important, the productivity is materially higher.
Japanese plants, most of which have been built since the
1950's, are more efficient than many American plants, a few of
which date as far back as the turn of the century. During the
critical second half of the 1960's, man-hours needed to produce
a ton of steel in the United States remained almost constant,
while they declined by almost 50 percent in Japan. By 1968, the
output in tons per man year was about one third higher in
Japan than in the U.S.; by the mid-1970's it was about 80
percent higher.

And why did the American steel industry, which in 1950

accounted for 47 percent of the world's steel production, fall behind technologically? To achieve maximum production requires huge investments in the most modern machinery. To make these investments, the industry has to raise large amounts of capital, and in order to raise the additional capital it has to show satisfactory earnings. But as a result of government pressure which kept prices low, and labor demands which pushed up cost, steel profits have been unsatisfactory for more than twenty years. In 1976 profit margins in the steel industry were about 3.5 percent of sales and 8 percent of stockholders' equity, compared with 5.6 percent and 14.5 percent, respectively, for all manufacturers. Moreover, much of the capital available could not be invested to increase productivity, but had to be used to meet ever tighter environmental standards. While the U.S. was falling behind in technology, wages continued to rise. By 1970 labor cost per ton of steel was about 2½ times as high in the U.S. as in Japan.

When Edwin H. Gott started work for U.S. Steel in 1937 the *daily* wage was $5. When he retired in 1973 as Chairman of the Board, the *hourly* wage was $7.30, and during most of these 36 years management and labor, and government and industry regarded each other as adversaries. Almost every administration, from Roosevelt to Carter, found it expedient to attack the steel industry — until it is today one of the sick industries of the nation.

WHO GETS WHAT?

Yet, after more than a generation of almost constant conflict, the basic facts remain obscured both for the workers who are losing their jobs and for the general public which has to foot the bill. Cost-of-living escalator clauses provide union workers with a considerable degree of protection against the ravages of inflation, but not against unemployment. And this link between inflation and unemployment is not clearly understood by a large segment of the American people. Having protected themselves against the impact of inflation, the members of powerful unions are less concerned about inflation than they would be if their own real income was shrinking every month, as it is for an ever larger segment of the American people.

PROFITS vs. WAGES COST

But there is another reason for the fact that so many people fail to see the connection between an increase in wages in excess of a simultaneous increase in productivity, and the resulting rise in the cost of living. Many — probably most — Americans have a completely false idea as to who gets what share of the consumer dollar, and they somehow feel that business can pay higher wages and greater benefits — not to mention higher taxes — simply by reducing profits — "obscene" or otherwise.

According to a poll conducted by Opinion Research, 52 percent of the high school teachers questioned thought that the biggest portion of the National Income went to the "owners of business" in the form of profits and dividends. Higher salaries, wages and taxes could thus be paid by reducing the share of the "rich." Actually, 76.2 percent of the 1976 National Income went to public and private employees in the form of wages, salaries and benefits. Obviously, if everybody in the United States received a 29 percent pay increase, as did the White House staff, the members of Congress, and the top federal bureaucrats in 1977, costs, prices, taxes, deficits and the money supply would zoom upwards, because it would be impossible to squeeze a 29 percent pay increase out of the 23.8 percent of the National

Income now received by other than employees.

What is true of the nation as a whole, is also true — and even more so — of the corporate sector. How is the consumer dollar divided between the owners of business and labor? According to an Opinion Research poll, the majority of the American people believe that in a division of corporate profits between owners and workers, 75 percent goes to the owners in the form of profits and only 25 percent to the workers in the form of wages and benefits. In view of this widespread misconception regarding the size of corporate profits, it is not surprising that workers will be inclined to strike for a "more equitable" distribution of income, and that the general public will support the strikes.

The only way in which this perfectly natural reaction can be counteracted is for leaders in government and business to see to it that all Americans, and especially the union members, are made aware of the fact that wages plus benefits already account for more than 75 percent of the National Income, and for more than 90 percent of the divisible corporate income.

These figures have been published regularly on an annual basis since 1936, but they are, unfortunately, buried in a mass of other statistics, available only to those who already know how to dig them out. For 1976, the *Survey of Current Business*, published by the U.S. Department of Commerce, showed the following figures:

	Billions of Dollars	Percent of Divisible Income
Compensation of employees of all U.S. corporations	$657.9	90.1
Net profits (after taxes)	72.0	9.9
	$729.9	100.0

Until the great majority of the American people are aware of these facts, strikes will continue, especially in mass production industries where the companies can easily pass the excessive employment cost increases on to the customers — to the extent, of course, that the market and foreign competition permit. When customers rebel, or do not have the necessary purchasing power to pay the increase in prices, or foreign competitors gain a larger share of the American market, American workers lose their jobs.

IMBALANCES AND INEQUITIES

Thus inequities develop in the American economy. Big pay increases in mass production industries; heavy lay-offs and occasional cuts in take-home pay in some industries, such as the building trades; no pay increases — or increases which do not cover the rising cost of living — for many state, county and municipal employees; and growing impoverishment of the millions of Americans who must live on fixed incomes.

This leaves just one group of workers, those employed by the federal government, immune to the effects of inflation and the threat of unemployment. No matter how fast their pay and pensions rise, all they have to do is to raise taxes, run larger deficits, and create more fiat money. Between 1970 and fiscal 1977 the federal tax take rose by more than 107 percent, from $193 billion to $401 billion, while the money supply — currency, demand and time deposits — grew from $418 billion at the end of 1970 to over $876 billion by the end of 1978, or by more than 109 percent.

THE "OLD DREAM"

And this brings us back to President Carter's remark: "New Faith in an Old Dream." The "old dream" is in reality what UAW President Walter Reuther called "an old idea" as far back as 1946. The UAW was on strike against General Motors, starting in November, 1945 and lasting for four months. Yet despite the widespread bitterness, Reuther and other labor leaders recognized the basic truth about the relationship between wages and productivity. During a nationwide broadcast on the evening of January 19, 1946, in the midst of the strike, Reuther explained:

> Wages are limited by . . . the ability [of the corporation] to pay and by our ability to produce. This is nothing new. It's an old idea. It's just common horse sense.

And by "ability to pay" Mr. Reuther meant the ability of a company to grant what the union was demanding without raising prices to cover the increased labor cost. The strike was eventually settled for an increase of 18½ cents an hour, which at the time was a large amount, even though it may seem a puny figure compared with the wage increases now demanded — and obtained — by some unions. It was also much less inflationary than most present-day increases because man-hour productivity was rising fairly rapidly. Walter Reuther used to boil down his "ability to pay" concept to one short phrase: He was not interested, he said, in getting his members "the wooden nickels of inflation."

All this was before the merger of the CIO and the AFL. In 1945, the two were still separate organizations, and the UAW belonged to the CIO.

What did the AFL think of Reuther's "ability to pay" concept? Did the AFL approve of it? It not only approved of the concept, but believed that the UAW and other CIO unions had violated the principle by having demanded — and struck — for too much, when they held out and eventually got, the 18½ cents an hour pay increase. As the AFL put it:
INCREASE. As the AFL put it:

Our demands [meaning the demands of the AFL unions] were adjusted to the needs of the postwar conversion period, for we recognized that workers would benefit most by speeding the transition, so that the production per man hour would be increased and output of consumer goods would make up shortages and check inflation . . . Therefore, if we found employers unable to pay the full increase without breaking price ceilings, our unions accepted five cents, and ten cents in the spring, when industry had reached a larger production volume ....

Some unions outside the Federation [referring to the CIO unions] did not consider the needs of the reconversion. A series of strikes were called in which demands were set at 30 percent of $2 a day . . . The oil strike in mid-September was followed by strikes in automobiles, electric equipment, meat packing and other industries, culminating finally in the steel strike of January 1946, when the steel workers insisted on striking although they were offered a wage increase of 15 cents an hour. The President settled the steel strike by breaking the price ceiling of strategic commodity, arranging a steel price increase of $5 a ton or eight percent before the steel companies agreed to grant an 18½ cent pay increase.

This provision of paying wage increases by raising prices has had a disastrous effect on the entire economy . . . The living cost rise brings a serious loss to every one of the millions of persons who have invested their money in war bonds or other savings, and to everyone who depends for his living on a pension or social security .... These unions which broke price ceilings to get 18½ cents followed a short-sighted policy. Early in July their press statements claimed they had lost most of this increase by rising living costs, and they brought the same losses on all other workers. Had they been really willing to accept smaller increases and adjust their demands by genuine collective bargaining to industries' ability to pay, they would have been better off today and so would all American workers. And their members might have saved huge losses incurred in long strikes.

And who signed this document? The entire Executive Committee of the AFL, among them William Green, President, and even John L. Lewis, who had organized the CIO, but by 1946 was back in the AFL. Also signing was George Meany, then Secretary-Treasurer of the AFL, and now "Mr. Labor," the longtime head of the AFL-CIO.

Today, the "old idea" of the postwar years seems largely forgotten — and as a result unemployment is chronic and inflation rampant.

A RETURN TO THE "ABILITY TO PAY" PRINCIPLE

How can the "ability to pay" principle be restored?

By Law? In the United States and most other free nations all sorts of price and wage controls have been attempted: price ceilings, guidelines, wage freezes, presidential "jawboning." Always without success. Controls flounder along during wartime, as long as they are buttressed by rationing, no-strike pledges, and patriotism. But they never work for any length of time in peacetime in a democracy.

It is different, of course, in totalitarian countries. In the Soviet Union wages are controlled — wartime or peacetime — because goods and services are rationed by government-determined prices. Strikes are forbidden, and pay increases tend to be smaller than the increase in productivity.

But such a system is impossible in a free society. How then can the "ability to pay" notion be restored in the western democracies?

LET THE PEOPLE KNOW

Abraham Lincoln's advice, "Without the support of public opinion, nothing can be accomplished; with it, nothing can fail," applies today as it did more than a hundred years ago. There is just one word which should be added to Lincoln's advice: "informed" public opinion. Today American public opinion is completely uninformed concerning the "arithmetic" of business, and the situation is getting worse rather than better despite the tens of millions of dollars spent by various organizations and many corporations on what might be called "cosmetic advertising": a lot of sermonizing, many clever words, but few facts.

A few years ago, according to an Opinion Research poll, the majority of the American people believed that corporations averaged a profit of 20 percent on sales after taxes, or twice the ten percent which the people regarded as "fair." In 1979, according to other polls, the people apparently believed that corporations were making a profit of 33 percent, and the oil companies 61 percent. No wonder that the oil company unions demanded — and obtained — a nine percent pay increase.

WHAT ARE THE FACTS?

While the average customer thinks business is making a profit of 33 percent, the food chain stores, for instance, where the people buy their groceries, are lucky when they clear one percent on sales after taxes. They just don't have the "ability to pay" big wage increases without raising prices. But their employees don't know this, because their employers have never told them.

Worse yet, the majority of all corporations have not even told their shareholders how much they pay their employees in wages, salaries and benefits, either in the aggregate, or in comparison with their own after-tax profits.

They do, as they must, report to everybody how much their net profits and their dividends are. And in the case of large corporations these profits look pretty big. In some instances, they run into hundreds of millions of dollars, and thus conjure up dreams among employees as to how much their pay could be increased if the company would just be "fair."

The only answer to this is to let the employees know how much they are already getting, and how this compares with the net profits and dividends. While the majority of the American people believe that the employees of American corporations get only about 25 percent out of every divisible corporate income dollar, they receive in reality more than 90 percent.

Why is there such a monumental disparity between what the people believe, and the facts concerning such a vital matter?

Because the facts are buried in a mass of statistics, instead of being presented in a simple, graphic form that could be as easily read and understood as a cigarette commercial. If the President really expects rank-and-file union members voluntarily to settle for less than the 29 percent increase the top bureaucrats received, he must present to the American people the facts as they affect the nation as a whole — and he must present these facts intelligibly. Corporate chief executives should be just as forthright with the "arithmetic" of their own enterprises — which very few are. They should consider the phenomenal success of the handful of companies which have "leveled" with their workers and their shareholders.

THE TRW STORY

Back in 1939, Thompson Products (now known as TRW Inc.) decided, at my suggestion, to report their financial results to their employees in a simple graphic form. The company has continued the practice to the present time and during the past almost forty years has never experienced a strike even though the workers are unionized. Productivity and profitability have improved, and TRW has grown from a local Cleveland company with 16,000 employees to a world-wide enterprise with over 90,000 employees.

For 1974, for instance, TRW reported in a carefully worked out graphic presentation the following facts:

Total customer sales	$2,486,022,000
Of this the company spent for utilities, supplies, household expenses, materials, taxes and depreciation	1,318,231,000
Leaving:	$1,167,791,000
Of this income available for distribution labor received 91.3%	1,066,861,000
Leaving a "profit" of	$ 100,930,000
More than half of this "profit" was plowed back into the business	52,506,000

which left for the owners a net profit of just 4.7% of the amount divisible between workers and owners	$ 48,424,000

Every employee could thus clearly see that there was no sense in striking for a ten percent or even five percent increase in wages and benefits. If the company was forced by the union to pay a major wage increase this would mean that either the profits would be wiped out, which would lead to the closing of the least profitable facilities, and thus deprive some of the workers of their jobs. Or it would mean less money plowed back into the company's facilities which in due course would result in obsolescence, a decrease in the company's ability to compete, and eventually the closing of some of the plants.

THE IDEA SPREAD SLOWLY

Despite its obvious logic, the idea of telling the workers the facts spread very slowly. Only a few American companies have yet adopted it. On the other hand, in Britain, a Member of Parliament, Jill Knight of Birmingham, made a speech in 1972 in the House of Commons in which she recommended to British industrialists the approach which TRW had used so successfully since 1939. Her advice was followed by Guest Keen & Nettlefolds, which has 75,000 employees in 350 factories scattered throughout the United Kingdom.

Like TRW, GKN, too, has had no more strikes since they showed their workers clearly how much of the divisible income the workers already received. And no wonder, for their graphic report for 1975, for instance, showed that the employees received 95 percent of each pound which was split between employees and owners, with net profits constituting the remaining five percent.

AUSTRALIA ADOPTS THE SAME POLICY

When the GKN "miracle" became known in Australia, where strikes were rampant and where employees' compensation had climbed by 70 percent during three years, while man-hour productivity had increased by less than one percent, I was invited to Australia to explain to the Prime Minister and to mass meetings in all major cities, how Britain's GKN had used the "arithmetic" of its business to end labor strife. There was no objection from anyone to the suggestion that Australian corporations simply "tell the truth, the whole truth and nothing but the truth" about how the available income is divided between aggregate employee compensation on the one hand and net profit after taxes on the other.

One of the first Australian companies to adopt the GKN policy was Arnotts Limited which presented its income figures in a graphic format suggested by Enterprise Australia, a non-profit economic educational foundation. This showed that a mere 5½ percent of the divisible income went to the owners in the form of dividends, while the workers received 88½ percent in wages and benefits, with the balance being plowed back into the business.

By 1977 more than 200 Australian companies had adopted the policy of "telling the full truth" — while in the United States, which has 200 million more people than Australia, only a couple of companies do so. Yet American companies, large and small, cannot plead "inability to pay" against excessive union demands, unless the financial realities are made abundantly clear to the millions of American workers and to the public at large.

Wage and benefit increases which by necessity must lead either to unemployment or to more inflation — to the detriment of a large minority, if not the majority, of the American people — can be stopped only if the public understands that in the long run neither a government nor a corporation can pay out more than it takes in. As Walter Reuther said — and George Meany agreed — it is just "common horse sense" that wage increases have to be governed by the "ability to pay," whether it be in the public or private sector. There is no sense in workers' striking for "the wooden nickels of inflation."

Yet today very few rank-and-file union members, and apparently very few union leaders, politicians and government officials seem willing to face these basic facts of economic "arithmetic."

VI

MINIMUM WAGES: UNEMPLOYMENT BY GOVERNMENT DECREE

John Chamberlain

The case against a compulsory minimum wage can best be established by asking a simple question: Who, in his right mind, will hire somebody to lose money for him? The man who can't earn his pay can hardly expect to retain sustained employment in marginal concerns that are having a difficult time making it, and even the firm that has a fat or a protected position is not likely to put up with losers on its payroll for long.

The purely logical case against the minimum wage was made as long ago as 1946 by George Stigler, the University of Chicago economist. At the time when Stigler was writing the basic minimum had just been changed from thirty to forty cents an hour. In view of the fact that the original Fair Labor Standards Act of 1938 gave coverage to only 43 percent of American workers, and this at a time when the approach of War was flushing payrolls everywhere as "Dr. New Deal" gave way to "Dr. Win-the-War," the overall effect of the minimum eluded easy correlations. As Finis Welch has pointed out in his monograph, "Minimum Wages: Issues and Evidence," there had been changes in teen-age employment in the 1930-40 decade. But in the depression years school enrollments rose, which meant that teen-agers weren't looking for steady work anyway. The war subsequently distorted all patterns as the military became the big employer.

The minimum wage might have hit hard if the postwar depression predicted by Henry Wallace had materialized in the months after Chester Bowles had closed down the Office of Price Administration. But the pent-up buying power accruing from forced wartime savings mocked the Wallaces and the Bowleses and the other doom-sayers. At a time when the tides were unpredictable, Stigler was right to rest his case on the common sense of classical, or Austrian, economics: other things being equal, it is unit productivity that governs the hiring of the marginal man.

Since Stigler's day, correlations have come more easily. From 1950 on, the politicians, reacting to the inflationary trends which they themselves had done so much to create, kept revising the minimum upwards at steadily shrinking intervals. In the Fifties the minimum was jumped twice, hitting a $1-an-hour rate in 1956. In the Sixties there were four changes, reaching $1.60 an hour in 1968. In 1974 the $2 basic minimum was established; three years later the figure had risen to $2.65. And on January 1, 1979, the new minimum was $2.90, with changes set at $3.10 and $3.35 for 1980 and 1981. Meanwhile more and more types of work had been brought under the official coverage, and the states have set their own minimums, sometimes even exceeding federal rates. The minimums have outpaced hourly increases in productivity, and this has made all the difference.

Yale Brozen, Stigler's University of Chicago colleague, has been able to find plenty of empirical evidence to back up the classical logic that tells you that an official floor is merely a statement to workers that unless they can find jobs at the minimum they will not be permitted to work. The minimum wage mandates unemployment.

Few people want to believe the empirical evidence, even though it has been set forth in statistical form by Yale Brozen, by Masanori Hashimoto, by Jacob Mincer and by Hyman Kaitz of the Department of Labor. In 1948, before the real increments in the minimum started to snowball, black youth unemployment was more or less the same as white youth unemployment. Indeed, for 1948, black youths aged 16-17 had an unemployment rate that was less than whites of the same age — 9.4 percent compared to 10.2 percent, as set forth by the Temple University economist Walter E. Williams, one of the leading black authorities in the field. But by 1976 the 16-17 black youth participation rate was running at slightly more than one-half that of white youths. It was a rout.

Since correlations overlap, and since they involve much confusion between causes and effects, commentators resist the conclusion that teen age unemployment in general, and black teen age unemployment in particular, can have an economic reason. The skeptics insist there must be some sort of social discrimination involved. In four articles by four separate reporters beginning on March 11, 1979, *The New York Times* tried to discover why a decade of civil rights enforcement has not solved the problem of growing black unemployment. John Herbers blames the trend on major changes in society, its structure and its political climate. There is (1) the influx of aliens taking the available jobs. There is (2) the entry of white women — representatives of the two-job family — into the job market. There is (3) the rise of the so-called underground economy — dope pushing, prostitution, gambling, mugging, robbing, living in jail at the expense of the public. There is (4) the movement of jobs out of the central city, where blacks are left behind. There is (5) the big change in agriculture, leading to disemployment on the farms that has not been compensated for by a willingness on the part of labor construction unions to make room for black apprentices. In addition to all this there is the general problem of a fractured society in which discrimination lingers and the taxpayers are not willing to pay for enough federal programs to reach and train the needy.

The failure, so the *Times'* Thomas Johnson says, is compounded by the "declining productivity of urban areas as the energy and skills of an entire layer of the community are left out." Industry doesn't want to locate in "unlivable" places. So these are left for the criminal to exploit. It isn't so much an inability of the young in the "unlivable" city to earn the minimum wage, it is their inability to find a way to the ever-more-distant factory door. Pushing marijuana is easier.

Then there is the "counter-productive" atmosphere created by our welfarist emphasis on federal and state programs of training and government-created jobs. It is easier to get along by invoking continued welfarist attention than it is to carry dishes in a university restaurant or to take a job as a messenger. The Comprehensive Employment and Training Act, CETA, leads to general dissatisfaction with the actual jobs that are available for low pay in the actual job market. We spend $40 billion in a decade on programs and when the beneficiaries go out into the real world "the job," to quote Professor Sar A. Levitan of George Washington University, "is not there." What has been learned is "not transferable."

No doubt practically everything the *Times* reporters and the scores of "authorities" they quote say is true. But how much of it is secondary to the main cause of interfering with the market processes that work, say, in Hongkong, where there is no minimum wage and little welfare? The *Times* series makes two mentions of the minimum wage only to denigrate it as a cause. The first is by John Herbers, author of the lead article, who quotes economists who say it is not "a major factor" in promoting unemployment. The second comes in article four, by Robert Reinhold, who says that a Joint Economic Committee of Congress study supported Walter Williams, the Temple economist (not mentioned as being a black himself) "echoes the business viewpoint" in saying "a lowered wage for teen-agers" would help. Mr. Reinhold's subsequent statement, that "the Administration is banking heavily on the new employment tax credit" to create apprentice jobs, constitutes an unconscious admission that "the business point of view" is something more than pure prejudice. So why wasn't more attention paid to Walter Williams in the *Times* series?

Professor Williams, contemplating the young black who can't get into a construction union or buy a truck to compete with a trucking association that has a certificate of convenience from the Interstate Commerce Commission, says, with an air of wistfulness, that the older minorities — the Irish, Poles, Italians, even the Chinese and Japanese — were lucky. They came here before there were any minimum wage laws. The blacks in the northern cities, the Latins (Puerto Ricans and Mexicans), came too late to be "melted," economically speaking. Professor Williams, in his own notable study which appeared in the Heritage Foundation's "Policy Review" for the Fall of 1977, mixes the econometric approach with sound reminders that economics is a study of the allocation of scarce resources. Choices, he says, must be made, since there isn't enough of everything to go around. The Law of Demand decrees that "whatever quantity of any good purchased at any particular price, a sufficiently higher price will induce any person to purchase less." So, under the Law of Demand, a minimum wage — a "sufficiently higher price" — will cause the employer to turn to labor-saving machinery, or to discontinue unprofitable lines of percentages altogether.

Congress can set the official wage, but it cannot in the nature of things legislate a productivity increase or force a labor transaction to be made.

The AFL-CIO's George Meany likes the minimum wage laws precisely because it eliminates, say, three low-skilled workers who are ready to do a job at less total outlay than would otherwise be paid to a high-skilled worker, so that the union can then step in and negotiate an even higher wage for the high-skilled operative. The effect of the minimum, says Williams, is to price the competition of the high-skilled to the workers out of the market. The unions, to make sure that the unemployed who can't earn the minimum wage will not become a "dangerous political powder keg," take the "humanitarian" stance of supporting such things as the Food Stamp Program, the Job Corps, Summer Work Programs and other "income subsidy programs." Of course, all this helps fuel the inflation that ultimately destroys the value of the high wage that Mr. Meany, with the help of the minimum wage laws, has negotiated.

Professor Williams cites Gramlich's Law that shows a 25 percent minimum wage increase lowers the employment of low wage youths by 10 to 15 percent. The outcome of Gramlich's Law is to offer the taxpayer a choice. Either he can support compensating massive federal make-work programs or he can face the consequences when discouraged and desperate jobless youth turn to anti-social activities in the underground economy.

No doubt the skeptics will continue to disregard the statistical correlations invoked by Walter Williams, Yale Brozen and others to show that increased unemployment follows legislated jumps in the minimum wage. In the skeptics' estimation it is just a matter of post hoc, ergo propter hoc, and hence a fallacy. But if the skeptics won't accept statistical indications, maybe they will listen to the candid admissions of a big employer. In a notable interview in *Fortune* magazine for January 29, 1979, I. Willard Marriott Jr., the president and chief executive of the big hotel and restaurant chain, says the recent Congressional action in raising the minimum to $2.90 an hour, with projected further jumps to $3.35 in 1981, has wiped out some 1,500 jobs in his company. Well before Congress had actually established the new base rates, Marriott called in productivity specialists to analyze how managers in each hotel and restaurant unit were utilizing and scheduling labor. Following the recommendations of the specialists, Marriott "eliminated more than two million man-hours, or about five percent of the total." It also stopped hiring at certain locations.

How did Marriott cut its work force by two to three percent without losing too many customers? In some cases it closed parts of a restaurant, opening one dining room instead of two. It accelerated the shift to self-service salad bars. It had to increase prices by ten percent in some restaurants to absorb the new minimums paid to workers who still held the marginal jobs. And, as might have been expected, the increased food prices led to a cyclical decrease in jobs.

Mr. Marriott offered *Fortune* a concrete example. Marriott used to have some twenty restaurants in the District of Columbia. The District has, traditionally, had one of the highest minimum wage levels in the United States. The cost of wages in the Marriott restaurants is the highest cost of their continuation in business. During the past three or four years, says Mr. Marriott, as the minimum kept advancing, his company has had to close fourteen restaurants and "terminate" 1,300 people, about a third of whom were minority youths.

What happened at Marriott was paralleled by a similar trend in other restaurant chains. The National Restaurant Association, surveying 2,000 of its members, found that after the minimum wage had been increased in 1978, ninety-five percent of them had had to raise prices and reduce man-hours. Some sixty percent of the restaurants laid off people, and more than half purchased new equipment that would help them reduce their labor force. Mr. Marriott, in citing these statistics, remarked humorously that it's hard to automate restaurants and hotels when you can't find a machine to make the beds.

In default of machinery, restaurants and hotels have to regard waitresses, who used to be specialists, as all-purpose human machine tools. In the past, a waitress only waited on tables. Now she cuts pies, makes the milkshakes and sodas, and clears the tables. This enables management to get rid of fountain boys and bus boys — usually teen-agers who have, traditionally, been hired at the minimum.

No doubt, says Mr. Marriott, if there were not a "maintenance-level minimum" to protect people against unscrupulous employers, there would be some "exploitation" in the economy. But when Mr. Marriott says he would hire quite a few more people for $2.30 an hour, the resultant expansion of jobs to include people who are not, at the moment, working at all could hardly be called exploiting anybody. A minimum, says Mr. Marriott, should take into account the different characteristics of different regions — and in southern cities, where heating bills are negligible, a $2.30 base pay would, actually, be the equivalent of a higher base in colder climes insofar as personal satisfactions are concerned. A wage differential for teen-age apprentices or tax rebates to companies for employing more people in the 17-21 age brackets would help solve some problems. But Mr. Marriott doubts that a Congress listening to the "drumbeat" of the labor unions will do anything about wage differentials in an election year.

What is needed, journalistically speaking, is a multiplication of studies to cover the many types of industry in our pluralistic economy. If a hundred business men would describe their hiring practices in the realistic terms that Mr. Marriott has supplied for *Fortune* magazine, it might convince the skeptics who scoff at post hoc statistical correlations. The case study is always more dramatic than a manipulation of statistical tables.

The trouble with statistics is that you don't see faces. But when you watch a hard-pressed waitress dashing from her table to run the fountain service and to clean up the coffee cups, the lesson of the compulsory minimum wage is rammed home.

VII

UNIONS, EMPLOYMENT AND PUBLIC ORDER

John A. Davenport

In the closing hours of the 95th Congress, the Carter Administration managed to push through a version of the much debated Humphrey-Hawkins bill which among other things commits the government to trying to reduce unemployment, then running at about 6% of the labor force, to a level of 4% by the year 1982. Much might be said against the government of a free society taking on any commitment as regards maintaining employment at a specific level, especially given the inadequacy of official statistics. Still more might be said against the general philosophy of Humphrey-Hawkins, which as originally drawn contemplated a large measure of statist planning.

My purpose here is to begin with a different issue and paradox. It is conceded that Humphrey-Hawkins could never have been passed without the constant lobbying of the A.F.L.-C.I.O. in particular and of organized labor in general. Yet examination will show that organized labor itself is a potent

cause of, though not the sole cause of, persistent unemployment which it then asks the government to cure through
increased spending, easy credit, and other measures that are
supposed to create jobs in the economy but which all too often,
as at present, lead on to perpetual inflation.

This statement will no doubt offend champions of what is
sometimes called the Labor movement and even may surprise
many who tend to be critical of unions. In the view of many
laymen, not to mention businessmen, labor unions are
dangerous because in raising costs they inevitably lead on to
rising prices. In fact, a rise in labor costs cannot by itself
produce a rise in the general price level. Inflation is uniquely
due to the issue of too much money chasing too few goods, and
labor unions do not and cannot issue money. What they may
do, through strike action, and through excessive wage and
benefit demands is to cut down on employment opportunities
in the economy, leading to a situation where the government
feels called upon to set the printing presses rolling.

Until recently it was generally held that such government
action could countervail the adverse effects on employment
which unions generate, and that increased government
spending to this end and to further all kinds of social programs,
which union leaders generally favor, would have no untoward
consequences. We are now learning to our cost that this is not
the case. Far from there being a trade-off between inflation
and unemployment, the one contributes to the other, yielding a
kind of stagflation where rising prices and unemployment go
hand in hand — the worst of all possible worlds.

THE PREMISE OF UNIONISM

In this situation it behooves us to take a hard look at
unionism in its present form, to canvass means of reforming it,
and to examine the central ideas that lie behind it, for as the

late Richard Weaver was wont to say: "Ideas have consequences." The central idea behind modern union organization is that men need some kind of collective organization to protect their rights and further their interests; and this need became increasingly manifest with the development of the modern factory system bringing large numbers of workers together in the pay of enlarging business enterprises. In this context the union is an organic growth from capitalism itself; and were unions purely *voluntary* associations, like a club or like a business corporation, they would pose no challenge to the market economy and the free society. On the contrary they would be welcome as an instrument for mediating between the complementary interests of workers and management, of working out differences sure to arise on the factory floor, and of giving workers a sense of "belonging" to our modern and often depersonalized industrial system, and lending needed ballast to the Ship of State.

But if such voluntary conditions ever existed in the distant past when unions, building on the old guild system, set out to better the lot of industrial workers, they have long since vanished as the result of legislation which gives unions unique power and privileges. Under present national law employers are *forced* to bargain with unions whether or not they believe this is to the interest of themselves or their workers. In addition a union gains exclusive bargaining rights in a plant or bargaining unit if it commands a bare majority of those voting and present, forcing the perhaps 49% minority to accept its services in wage and other negotiations whether they desire such services or not. Finally unless prevented by state Right-to-Work legislation, unions can and do draw contracts with employers which make union membership or at least payment of union dues the price of keeping a job, and such dues more often than not are then used for political purposes.

Still more decisively the modern union uses methods and

tactics for enforcing its demands which differ *toto caelo* from those used by any other form of business or business agency. Its chosen instrument is the strike, reinforced by the picket line (both, incidentally, military terms) which represent far more than a collective withdrawal of services or mass resignation. The objective of the strike is to close down the employer's facilities until he accepts union terms, at which point most strikers expect and do get their jobs back. The objective of the modern picket line is not just to advertise a strike (in which case a single picket carrying a placard would be sufficient). *It is to prevent other workers, who may desire to accept the employer's terms, from working.* The result is that so-called collective bargaining becomes a form of collective clobbering, driving a deep wedge between the mutual and complementary interests of labor and capital, and in so far as it is accompanied by violence and threats of violence, undermining the sovereign power of government to maintain order.

THE STRIKE THREAT SYSTEM

It is sometimes argued that these untoward effects of industrial warfare cannot be too great because unions today command a bare 25% of the U.S. working force, and a declining share at that, and because in a better than $2-trillion economy the unemployment effect of strike action is bound to be minimal in terms of man-days of work lost vs. total man-days worked. It would be foolhardy to take too much comfort from such statistics. The prolonged coal strike the winter of 1977-78 idled not only thousands of miners but had a ripple effect through all coal-dependent industries. In years past strike action has closed down our steel and automobile plants for months at a time. It was the perception of the late Robert Kennedy that the Teamsters have the power to tie up the country's transportation facilities overnight. A multitude of craft unions

— carpenters, plumbers, steam fitters, etc., can and do harass the construction industry and the recent New York newspaper strike idled some 10,000 employees. Finally, unionism has made its most spectacular gains of recent years among government workers and civil servants, with the result that teachers periodically close down our public schools, and that firemen and even policemen can leave whole cities unprotected.

Moreover, strike action is only the tip of the iceberg in evaluating the adverse effects of union tactics. Of far greater importance is the *threat* of such action in the collective bargaining process. Such threat gives unions enormous power over the economy, and this power may be greatest where labor relations appear on the surface to be most peaceful. In effect the strike threat puts productive investment at risk, and retards and distorts capital formation which is essential for economic growth and the key factor in raising *real* wages and living standards for all. The true interests of labor and capital, far from being opposed, are in fact complementary and neither can get along without the other. Indeed economic progress depends precisely on the development of better tools and machines which increase worker productivity and hence real output. Creative investment by entrepreneurs is the heart and sinew of this process.

The strike threat is an open challenge to such investment. It is most serious in industries such as steel or railroads which involve huge "sunk costs" in the form of plant and equipment which in one way or another must be paid for over long periods of time, and which involve overhead charges that continue whether the plant is operating or not. Faced with potential strike action the owners and managers of such facilities are apt to settle for union demands, bearing little relation to productivity, rather than risk a shutdown. Meanwhile new investment will avoid such industries like the plague and will flow towards less tightly organized enterprises where risks are lower. The country may need, and in fact today does need, the renovation of its steel mills. It may get instead a plethora of gambling casinos which however hazardous involve relatively low sunk costs and unlike a steel mill may be conveniently moved from place to place as labor exigencies require.

HIGHER WAGES & FEWER JOBS

This inhibiting and distorting effect on private investment may well be the most serious threat which unions pose to the goal of maintaining high employment levels. It is, of course, not the only threat. For one must furthermore take into account what happens when unions win their outside demands, and here a whole mythology must be challenged. It is the claim of many union leaders that their organizing efforts have benefited not just union members but the entire working class. This claim may be rejected out of hand. Real wages (wages discounted for inflation) began to rise in this country as well as others long before unions became powerful and did so precisely as the result of capital accumulation and the progress of invention. Moreover the level of real wages and incomes in different countries bears no relation whatever to the degree they have been unionized. England, for instance, trails far behind the United States though it is the home of the modern union movement.

Finally, and disturbingly for union claims, the *share* of national income going to wages and salaries, and the share going to other forms of income such as interest, profits, and rents, has remained remarkably constant over long periods of time. The idea that unions can benefit *all* workers by wresting rewards from greedy capitalists is without foundation. Indeed, Nobel Prize winner F.A. Hayek has argued that the rise of powerful unions has probably adversely affected real wages for the working class taken as a whole.

What unions are able to do is, through use of the strike and the strike threat, to raise *money* wages, and sometimes real wages for *particular groups* higher than they otherwise might have been. By how much unions can do this is subject to considerable economic dispute, since it is always difficult to prove through statistics the difference between what actually occurs and what might have been the case in other circumstances. Working with studies by Gregg Lewis and Charles Riess, as well as his own calculations, Milton Friedman has hazarded the guess that unions over time have raised wages for part of the working force by some 15%. This seems an extraordinarily conservative estimate, and the effect of unionization in trucking and in the building trades, to mention but two industries, is undoubtedly much higher.

What is not open to question is that any benefits which unions achieve for their members are taken out of the hides of *other* workers, since as noted the share of national income going to wages and salaries for all workers has tended to remain more or less constant. And what is furthermore not open to question is that in so far as unions have achieved higher rewards for their members, they have had a disemployment effect in the industries in question. The dramatic rise in wages in soft coal mining after World War II, and the accompanying drop in employment is a case in point. The late John L. Lewis is reputed to have said that his objective was to make "every miner a king" but he neglected to say *how many* miners were to achieve this kingly status. The evidence indicates that as wages in any trade are pushed up beyond where the free market would put them there will be decreasing employment opportunities as employers hasten to mechanize their operations or as capital shifts away from the industries in question. This, after all, conforms to common sense observation. We all know that in the matter of remuneration we are foolish if we do not ask for as much as the market will bear. But we also know that if by chance we demand, say, a doubling in wage or in salary and win it, the comfortable occupation we are in may disappear entirely. In short, unions can and do price workers out of jobs.

Were the labor market for the economy as a whole perfectly flexible and fluid the action of unions might not have permanent effect on employment taken as a whole. But the market, of course, is not perfectly fluid. Displaced workers cannot easily pack up their belongings and move into other industries. Hence pockets of unemployment are created when wages are pressed too high: witness conditions in New England as textiles moved South, and in Johnstown, Pa. when Bethlehem Steel decided to close down its facilities there entirely. More broadly, the effect of unionization is to restrict job opportunities in the higher paying trades, forcing men down the ladder into less remunerative occupations. This crowding down effect means that more men and women must seek employment towards the bottom of our society. But as this bottom is reached there is an ultimate road-block to any employment at all. It takes the form of minimum wage laws which unions have always strongly favored not because they directly benefit their own members but because they prevent the undermining of the wage structure by non-unionized workers.

The evidence is now overwhelming that when minimum wage floors are raised unemployment tends to increase for the less fortunate members of our society; and the effect of minimum wages perfectly illustrates the fact that wages are a form of price, and that when this price is tampered with the result will be a decrease of demand. The process, be it noted, is especially unfair to the poorest members of the community who are denied the dignity of work and are driven onto the welfare rolls and supported out of the taxpayer's pocketbook. Far from remedying poverty, union pressures for high wages in the tightly organized industries, combined with the minimum wage laws, have probably increased poverty, and certainly have increased the load which government now bears for caring for the destitute and dispossessed.

THE KEYNESIAN SUBTERFUGE

This load is not inconsiderable as the condition of New York City dramatizes where welfare payments of one kind or another run to over $1 billion per year or over one seventh of the city's budget. But welfare in the restricted sense of the word, meaning relief for the destitute is, of course, only a small fraction of the total load which American citizens now pay for so-called "public welfare spending" defined as any government payment directly benefiting the recipient including such massive programs as Social Security, Medicare, Medicaid, Unemployment benefits, aid to education, government pensions and veterans benefits. In 1975 such spending ran at all levels of government to a colossal $287 billions, and now constitute well over 50% of the federal budget as the American version of the Welfare State has flowered and, in many cases, run wild. It is these mounting "transfer payments" which more than anything else today account for huge federal deficits and for inflation, and in this whole area organized labor, acting in its *political* capacity as a lobbying interest group, has played a decisive though not an exclusive role from the days of the New Deal forward.

This propensity of Labor to back almost any measure labelled as contributing to the public welfare is in part attributable to benevolent motives and in part to the notion that government spending and the pumping up of so-called "aggregate demand" will lead to more jobs and higher pay checks. This notion received powerful public support in the depression thirties as the result of the writings of John Maynard Keynes whose doctrines are subject to much misunderstanding by friend and foe alike. At the very opening of his celebrated *General Theory of Employment, Interest and Money*, Keynes asserts that he has no quarrel with the classical position which held that the remuneration of workers should conform to their marginal product, and even went on to say that in the short run, and barring capital development, "an increase in employment can only occur to the accompaniment of a *decline* in the rate of real wages." Such decline, however, can be accomplished in two different ways. One might be the cutting of money wages or at least the arresting of their continuous advances. The other would be to raise prices of products *faster* than nominal wages through increased government outlays. Such reflation Keynes argued would reduce real wages for the time being while leaving money wages untouched. The result would be a restoration of profits and the rejuvenation of investment without the costly and unpopular business of wage renegotiation.

In effect the Keynesian cure for depression and recession involved playing a kind of trick on workers through a species of sleight-of-hand. Unfortunately for theorists, union leaders were quick to see through this subterfuge. During the depression Thirties enlarged government spending was gingerly tried out but never restored anything like full employment, partly because the New Deal continued to beat businessmen over the head for their alleged sins, partly because this was a period of rapid increase in unionization accompanied by much industrial warfare, and partly because wages, both nominal and *real* rose more rapidly than at any previous time in our history. In the post World War II era we have become accustomed to big government budgets and deficits, largely as the result of welfare measures, and in the Fifties and early Sixties the trio of Big Government, Big

Business and Big Labor seemed to have found a modus vivendi without undue inflationary pressures. But of more recent years from roughly 1965 forward this dispensation has tended to unravel, giving rise to periodic bouts of stagflation where prices, wages, and unemployment may rise together. Far from stimulating real output and jobs, inflation becomes counter-productive.

The reasons are not far to seek. As Milton Friedman has astutely pointed out inflation can only increase employment opportunities in so far as it is *unanticipated.* Where it is anticipated by trade union leaders, and indeed by all classes of society, it results only in a mindless spiraling of both prices and costs with no net effect on job opportunities and in practice a negative effect. For inflation upsets all business calculations for the future and in so doing restrains long term investment. It also, like the minimum wage, bears heaviest on the poor and dispossessed who are least able to protect themselves from its ravages. In effect inflation as the result of government spending becomes the cruelest and most debilitating tax of all.

THE ROAD TO REFORM

The challenge now facing the U.S., as well as many other Western democracies, is how they can arrest this process, and two different approaches present themselves. The first, succumbed to by the Carter Administration, is to attempt to control prices and wages by voluntary guide-lines and "standards" or by resort to mandatory controls, which the A.F. of L.-C.I.O favors. This is a disquieting development since controls are the downhill road to complete government domination of the economy if not to the collectivist state.

The second and indeed the only effective course is to get at the roots of inflation not just by stringent credit policy, which bears hardest on the private sector of the economy, but by budgetary restraint. In a wintry and dangerous world there is no chance of cutting military expenditures and, indeed, they should probably be increased. What calls for pruning are precisely those mounting welfare and transfer payments which organized labor, as well as other pressure groups, have always favored. For it is these which lie at the heart of our difficulties.

Yet if fiscal restraint and tax reduction are to succeed, if the dollar is to be restored as a world currency, then I submit that something more is needed — namely to restore initiative and incentive within the private sector of the economy itself. Sound money and open markets for goods, labor and capital are complementary to each other. With respect to business we are protected by the Sherman Act and by other anti-monopoly laws. In the field of labor we have sowed the whirlwind by granting to unions exemptions and privileges that no private group should enjoy. The need here, let it be said in the beginning, is not for more and ever more complex labor legislation of which we already have too much. The need is to enforce certain general prohibitions already on the books while modifying other laws which never should have been passed in the first place in their present form.

As an example of the first objective the primary aim of labor reform should be to enforce to the letter both federal and state legislation, as well as common law practice, which aims to eliminate all forms of violence, overt or covert. The tragedy of our times is that such measures are not being enforced especially in the case of strike action and mass picketing. If during a maritime strike one should go down to the waterfront to seek a job it would presumably not be a striker who would hit one over the head. It would in all probability be a New York City policeman swinging his night stick. As a classic example of this misuse of the police power let me recall a strike at

General Electric of some years ago where the Electrical Workers threw up a picket line around that company's huge facilities at Schenectady. In this case, far from dispersing the pickets, the Schenectady local police and city authorities actually pleaded with independent workers *not* to try to cross the picket line lest the effort might result in mayhem and bloodshed! It would be hard to find a better case for illustrating how far the administration of the law now winks at union violence and threat of violence. And violence in all its forms is a disgrace to the high professions of the union movement no less than to a country dedicated not just to liberty but to *liberty under law.*

Secondly, and directly relating to the containment of violence when it does flare, it is time that we returned to the ancient common law principle that every man and every institution deserves his "day in court." This principle was breached by the Norris-La Guardia Act of 1932 which made it practically impossible for employers or individual workers to obtain temporary injunctive relief when attacked by union thugs and bullies. As that great labor student, Sylvester Petro, has argued such temporary injunctive relief was not a way of smashing unions, as the late Supreme Court Justice Felix Frankfurter so perversely held. It was rather a way by which companies and individuals could obtain a temporary stay, or a "still pond no more moving" edict, against the destruction of life and property until their tempers had cooled and due process of law could weigh the facts of the situation. As of today such protection has been nullified by a mountain of "administrative law" as interpreted by the National Labor Relations Board. From its decisions appeal can still be made to the courts. But by the time such appeal has been made and has ground through judicial process the adversely affected party to a strike has in most cases lost the ball game. As one small employer put it to the McClellan Committee many years ago:

"I never lost a case before the N.L.R.B. but I did lose my business!"

FREEING THE FREE RIDER

These two measures — the enforcement of laws against violence and the restoration of temporary injunctive relief to both employees and employers — would in and by themselves go far to curb union excesses. Perhaps they are all that is needed, anyway, as a first step. On longer term, however, we should re-examine the provisions of the Wagner Act of 1935 which even as amended by Taft-Hartley gives unions extraordinary privileges. For not only does it *force* all employers at pain of extinction to the bargaining table but so far as unions are concerned it contradicts its own premises. In Section 7 it proclaims as basic principle that all wokers shall have the right to join unions *or not*, and engage in union activities *or not* as they may so desire. It then, as noted in the beginning, gives unions *exclusive* bargaining privileges on the basis of a bare majority and permits, unless barred by State action, the drawing of union shop contracts which force all workers to pay union dues regardless of their wishes. This loophole in the law is really the converse of the old Yellow Dog contract which allowed employers to bar all forms of union organization. It is sometimes justified by the argument that without forced union organization there would be many "free riders" who would benefit from union bargaining without payment for it. But surely the simpler way of eliminating the "free rider" would be to rescind the whole exclusive bargaining privilege. In this case the whole free rider argument collapses. Those who wanted union representation would get it. Those who did not want it would bargain for themselves.

This reform particularly commends itself since it would be a first and decisive step toward making unions conform to the law of agency as it pertains to most other departments of our economy. Such agencies — vide the real estate agent or the literary agent — have a useful place in a free society as paid professional bargainers. But what would one think of a literary agent who insisted that all writers be members of his organization whether they wished his services or not? Or of the real estate agent who declared that because 51% of the householders on a block or in a district chose his representation, all others should do likewise? It is precisely because unions pose as agents of the working man, yet breach the fundamental law of agency that they raise such an intractable problem. A true agent, for instance, is always suable for malfeasance in the courts of law. Such suits can in some instances be brought against unions but they are relatively few and far between. Progress in domesticating unions will be made as they become amenable to criminal and civil action both by their members and by the public at large whose interests in maintaining services, — transportation services, for instance — are today completely disregarded with no legal means of redress.

It will be argued that union reform along the lines indicated above would mean the elimination of unions entirely and returning the worker to a form of industrial slavery. Such arguments must be taken with a large grain of salt. It is worth recalling that in 1920, long before the passage of Norris-La Guardia in 1932 and the Wagner Act in 1935 there were some 5,000,000 union members who seemed to get along without these laws. It is also worth emphasizing that today 75% of the U.S. working force earns its way without any unionization at all and that many companies, who at most have small voluntary unions restricted to the enterprise in question, pay *higher* wages than in the heavily organized sectors of the economy where unions are industry-wide. In an industrialized society there will always be room for worker associations since birds of a feather flock together and, as noted in the beginning, such association may do much to better conditions on the factory floor, to restrain over-arrogant supervisors, and in general to mediate between management and employees. What is not true is that without big monolithic unions all wages would collapse to subsistence levels or worse. What sustains wages is the fact that the owners and managers of capital need workers as much as workers need tools to work with, and that advance in both real wages and living standards is uniquely geared to capital investment.

THE MAN AND THE LAWN MOWER

This brings me in conclusion to stress two points — one economic and the other political — where there is wide public misunderstanding of the process which sustains our society — a misunderstanding which needs correcting if we are ever to free ourselves of union excesses. The first related to the interdependence of labor and capital as distinguished from the war that is supposed to exist between them. There common sense is worth a good deal of theorizing. In cutting a lawn I invest in a lawn mower, a primitive form of capital. If I handle it properly I shall find at day's end that my lawn looks respectable. If I fight it I shall not get much grass cut and will probably get maimed in the process!

The point is well worth developing because union propaganda, and indeed common word usage, tends to cut the nexus of human work and capital, and to misrepresent the entire owner and managerial function. We speak of owners and their paid managers as "employing" labor. But in truth both are "employed" by a third party — namely the *consumer* who includes worker, manager, and just about everybody else. The businessman when all is said and done is not some kind of demigod enjoying an assured position in society in his own right.

The businessman is nothing more than a *middle-man*, mediating between the desire of the worker to better his condition, and the desire of the public for better and hopefully cheaper goods and services from tooth brushes to skyscrapers. If the businessman or capitalist judges the needs and tastes of the public correctly he makes a profit, but such profit is not ground out of the hides of employees as posited by Karl Marx in his mistaken theory of surplus value. It is rather the reward of *risk taking* of the kind that any store keeper takes when he stocks his establishment *before* a single customer appears. If he has judged the market correctly a margin of profit will show up on his books after all other expenses — wages, the costs of inventory, and rent — are paid. If he judges the market incorrectly, as apparently Abraham Lincoln did when in his early years he took to storekeeping, his penalty will be loss and eventually bankruptcy. We live not in a profit but in a *profit-and-loss* economy.

And precisely because this is the case the function of workers, and the function of entrepreneurs or owners, while complementary, cannot be transposed or merged into one. This becomes clear when we consider how often plans have been put forward whereby workers organized in unions would attempt to share in profit reward. Exercised within a single company, profit-sharing has much to be said for it as an incentive to better work and loyalty. But it should be noted that even here it is seldom carried to its logical conclusion — namely that when losses are suffered they would be docked from the employee's pay check. Carried out on a grander scale where all workers would share not only in profits but in losses as they occur, the idea of this kind of joint ownership of the means of production becomes wholly unacceptable, and union leaders would be the first to denounce it as exploitative. Modern society has found a way around this dilemma by a kind of division of labor as between employees, on the one hand, and managers and owners on the other. The first is *guaranteed* his pay check as long as he is employed and usually receives a number of weeks benefit in case of lay-off. The owner has no such guaranty of dividend return in good times or in bad. He has already sunk his capital into the venture and must take his chances as to profit or total loss. This would appear to be the fairest sharing of the productive burden that can be worked out. As W. H. Hutt has pointed out it means that those least able to bear the risks of capital development, and they are very considerable, do not have to take them, and that those most able to bear this risk assume what is by no means always a pleasant or a lucrative responsibility.

THE SYNDICALIST TRAP

Once this is realized, most union allegations that there is something inherently unfair in the capitalist process fall to the ground. But there is a second and no less potent challenge to our political economy which needs consideration and where once again there is widespread public misunderstanding. It is often averred that as matters are going the U.S. is in danger of socialization as the result of the ever-expanding power of the Welfare State to penetrate and influence our lives. There is no doubt that such threat does exist as government spending and regulation of prices and wages grows and multiplies. Yet in the U.S. at least union leaders are rarely exponents of pure socialist theory — meaning government ownership of the means of production. They correctly sense, and the historical record bears out their perception, that Socialism can no more tolerate unrestricted union power than can capitalism itself. There is no free trade union movement in Russia or in its satellite European states or in post-war China. And in foreign policy matters at least it is not happenstance that it was the A.F. of L.-C.I.O. which hailed the coming of Solzhenitzyn to this country while he was debarred entry to the White House.

But while opposing Socialism and Communism, American trade unionism, and indeed the American public, have been much less percipient in taking the measure of a different kind of threat to our institutions. This takes the form of private groups arrogating to themselves coercive powers which should properly belong to government and to government alone. As Irving Kristol acutely pointed out recently, trade unionism, in so far as it has ever had a political philosophy, is infected by the idea not of socialism but of an equally dangerous fallacy — namely the theory of Syndicalism. The essence of that theory, as developed in the nineteenth century, was that unionism in questing for every greater authority could take over not just the management of business enterprises but in the end take over functions now entrusted to government, making the whole apparatus of the modern state unnecessary. Exactly how this could benefit the worker and the world at large was never spelt out in detail, but the members of Syndicalism continue to smoulder in many union pronouncements and even more in union action and ambitions. As defined by the late great Samuel Gompers the aim of unionism is simply to get "more" out of the going economic system. But this "more" is subject to constant expansion in meaning and character. Yesterday it referred to better wages and salaries. Today it connotes more *Power*, political no less than economic. The U.S. has yet to undergo the traumatic experience of Sweden where some years ago clerks, judges, and even members of the armed services joined in mass protest against government authority. But clearly when firemen and policemen, prison guards and hospital attendants and teachers, engage in or threaten strike action against all the interests of the community, the elementary duty of government to protect the public interest is then threatened. A few steps further down this road lies the condition of modern Britain where trade unions, in full control of the Labor Party, again can freeze the country by a general strike, can pull down governments at will, and are today a clear and present danger to Parliamentary democracy.

FREEDOM & ORDER

There is no need for the U.S. to follow in Britain's footsteps but if this is to be avoided there *is* clear need to reassert the principles on which the American Republic was founded: namely that men are endowed with certain inalienable rights, and that governments are formed not to grant these, for they are inherent, but to nurture and protect them. In doing so government in the pungent phrase of the late Henry Simons is by its very nature the "final reservoir of coercive power," as seen in its policy power, and in the military establishment, and indeed in the case of the tax collector. But precisely because government is by nature coercive, its powers must be *limited* and jealously guarded. Our difficulties today stem largely from the fact that we have broken both rules. On the one hand, with the rise of the Welfare State we have given government far more functions than it can possibly handle. On the other hand, as in the case of unions in particular, the government has, so to speak, "farmed out" its coercive power to a private group which not only threatens the enterprise economy but also threatens the ability of the government to govern. It is in effect besieged by a species of war lords such as once led to the disintegration of China.

But what government has given it can also take away, and the task of true labor reform lies precisely in this direction. In the public sector this means the outright outlawing of strikes against the sovereign; in the private sector it means stripping unions of their monopoly of violence which in most cases makes strikes effective. The job that stretches ahead is therefore more basic than the conquest of inflation, the rehabilitation of the integrity of the dollar, and the conquest restoration of high employment levels. It is to restore constitutional *order* at home, without which all freedoms perish, while summoning the courage and the will to resist the spread of Soviet tyranny which has made no bones about its intention to bury us. The fundamental challenge was posed some two hundred years ago by that sage of common sense, Benjamin Franklin, who remarked at the conclusion of the Constitutional Convention: "We have given you a republic; it is for you to keep it."

VIII

SAVINGS, CAPITAL FORMATION, AND EMPLOYMENT

Patrick M. Boarman

Only about five percent of all the goods and services produced in the United States is directly the product of human effort. The other 95 percent is produced in roundabout fashion by inanimate power and machines. Without the modern tools of production, the standard of living of the American people would decline drastically. In the poorer countries, literally millions would perish for lack of food, shelter and other necessities. Moreover, without a constantly *growing* stock of capital (factories and machinery) the number of remunerative jobs available would lag behind the growing labor force, resulting in increasing chronic unemployment. In American industry, for example, it takes about $400,000 of new capital investment to create just one new job paying the average industrial wage. If the flow of capital investment is impaired, job opportunities at conventional or mandated wage levels would decline. While there are several forces which account for chronic unemployment in the United States, inadequate savings and its correlative, inadequate capital formation, are among the most important.

THE ORIGIN OF "CAPITAL"

In the dawn of man's existence, some millions of years ago, virtually all his time and energy were expended on merely keeping alive. Warding off the omnipresent threats of hunger, cold, disease, and attacks by animals and by other men, was a never-ending exercise. Life was — in myriad ways that have escaped any chronicling — undoubtedly "nasty, brutish, and short."

This lifestyle began to change significantly with the creation by homo sapiens of the first piece of capital. Imagine the event occurring eons ago. One of our ancestors, chronically hungry and cold and fearful, but a shade cleverer, perhaps, than his fellows, stands with his feet planted firmly in the middle of a shallow stream trying to catch the fish that go by with his bare hands. With luck he manages to catch enough in many hours of work to keep himself and his family going for another day. But then, on one memorable fishing venture, his eye is caught by a small hook-shaped bone, the relic of some dead animal. He's seized with a brilliant idea — for a fishing hook and pole!

Translating this idea into reality is not easy, however, for the time and energy required to fashion the pole is time and energy he cannot use to catch fish by the old method. The daily haul of fish, already meagre, will be reduced still further. In short, the formation of this piece of capital, which will greatly increase the catch of fish in the future, requires the cessation of consumption today. It requires *saving*.

As our primitive fisherman channels his time and energy into the production of the fishing pole, he is, in fact, investing, which is another way of saying that he is creating capital. He is at the same time saving, because without giving up some current consumption, he could not make the pole. Saving and investing, or saving and capital formation are two sides of the same coin.

The act of investment is the result of a deliberate choice to favor larger satisfactions in the future at the cost of reduced satisfactions today. Our fisherman is willing to endure the pangs of hunger today for the much larger harvests of fish he will be enjoying tomorrow and next week, and for many moons thereafter.

It is at this point that the law of capital accumulation — one of Karl Marx's better insights — begins to operate. Once production has increased in consequence of the use of the new tool, it becomes possible to accumulate a reserve stock of fish, cured by sun and salt, to be eaten by the family while the fisherman takes off a week from his fishing for the purpose of fashioning a bow and arrow, or a spear, to kill warm-blooded game. Not only does the margin for future consumption of goods rise, but there is increased variety in the diet and thus a real increase in the family's standard of living. In fact, the quantity of food may now expand to the point wherever larger quantities of it can be cured and stored, making possible the allocation of still more time and energy to the manufacture of new and more productive tools — a plough, perhaps a barn in which to preserve the multiplying crops. The point is, once that first step, the first act of self-denial and investment is made, the possibility of saving ever more and of investing ever more increases exponentially.

NO ECONOMIC GROWTH WITHOUT CAPITAL FORMATION

The troubling plight of many of the less-developed countries today is that they seemingly cannot or will not take that first step. As the well-worn cliche has it, they — the LDCs — are trapped (allegedly) in a "vicious circle of poverty," in which peoples' incomes are already so low that any attempt to extract savings from them would mean starvation and death. The developed countries on the other hand (some also call them the "rich" countries), having long since passed through the boundary at which savings entail severe hardships, appear to have entered a "virtuous circle" in which they more they have, the more they can accumulate, and the richer they become.

Needless to say, this dynamic, which tends to produce marked disparities of income and wealth, not only among countries butwithin a given country as well, is vastly irritating to legions of self-appointed custodians of "social justice." Viewing the gap between the haves and the have-nots as the product of an "imperialist conspiracy," or simply as the inherent attribute of a capitalist economy, they have over the last 200 years drawn up countless schemes for closing the gap. All these schemes, where they have been implemented, have had the effect of expropriating in greater or lesser degree from the clever, the bright, the productive, and yes the rich members of the society — the prime sources of savings — while increasing the consumption of the poor. While there is nothing wrong with increasing the consumption of the poor, indeed that is one of the prime accomplishments of modern capitalism, when it comes about at the cost of extinguishing the class of savers and entrepreneurs, everybody will be worse off in the future, including the poor and *especially* the poor. "Soaking the rich" to the point of eliminating them is, in the nature of the case, a one-shot operation. It is also a suicidal one in that it destroys the means whereby capital — the engine of progress — can be formed.

Great Britain, once the richest nation in Europe and the paradigm of a successful capitalist economy, is today the spectacular and dismaying example of the reduction in the economic well-being of everybody that social envy joined to economic know-nothingism can bring about. On the other hand, we have the example of the USSR, whose Communist overloads have, by force, extracted from the people savings they would not have yielded up voluntarily. The degree to which mass consumption can be restricted and capital goods increased in a totalitarian regime is impressive. For those who don't value freedom, there may be some lessons here. On the other hand, the perpetual postponement of consumption in such societies borders on the absurd, even on their own terms. What is the point of forming capital just for the sake of forming more capital?

To return to our fisherman: we need to ask under what social and economic and legal circumstances will he — valuing his freedom and able to exercise it — take that first step of making the fishing pole, and under what circumstances will he not do so? It is clear that he would not have endured the sacrifice and the hassle of saving to make the pole knowing in advance that most or even all of the extra fish he might catch would be confiscated by the chief of his tribe and, in the name of social justice, transferred to some poor and deserving fellow in the next hut (if you're poor, you're automatically deserving!).

Now if the chief had decided to leave the entrepreneurial fisherman with at least a portion of the increased catch of fish, he might still have made the pole but his enthusiasm for the undertaking of similar enterprises in the future would be sharply diminished. Not only that, but the very arbitrariness of the chief's behavior and, looking to the future, its associated unpredictability would substantially raise the risks of any future investments. While his own drive and innate talents as an innovator and doer might carry the primitive fisherman along for a while, the absence of any settled and permanent understandings about how and in what degree the results of his efforts would be distributed, indeed whether there would be any net rewards at all, would have a chilling effect on all his future saving and investment activities.

There is another thing the chief might do to make the "entrepreneur's" life difficult, for example, by requiring him to festoon his fishing pole with a leafy camouflage so as not to frighten the local frogs — deemed to possess occult powers over the village. He could also compel him to mark up a couple of dozen cuneiform tablets, spelling out when, where, and for how long he planned to do his fishing and what environmental impacts this new activity would be likely to have. Finally, he might instruct him to deliver up to the community (in the form of a tax) 20 of the 50 fish he had set aside in his food chest as a stock to live on during the time required to replace the fishing pole, now worn out, with a new one. However, with the 50 fish being the "capitalist" fisherman's realistic estimate of his food requirements during the period of manufacture, or of the cost, in fish, of having a friend make a new fishing pole for him, the replacement will appear unprofitable, or it will be postponed until the pole is so dilapidated that the amount of fish caught with it falls below his own previous average production. In effect, the chief's illiberal depreciation schedule has caused our fisherman's saving to fall below the replacement cost of his now worn-out capital. The result is that his living standard, as well as that of his tribe, inevitably declines.

There is a critical lesson here. The "vicious circle" in which some LDCs appear to find themselves, and in which some social groups within the U.S. claim to find themselves, is not inevitable and is not a consequence of capitalism, but of its absence. There is no question that in the LDCs, as Peter Bauer has made clear in his voluminous writings on the subject,[1] and in the urban and rural ghettos of the United States, many an enterprising fisherman can be found, capable of saving and investing if only given a chance, but whose potential for assuming such functions has been thwarted by attitudes hostile to thrift and to entrepreneurial success and envious of the rewards they bring.

THE SHORTFALL IN CAPITAL FORMATION

Beyond this, but in parallel with it, Americans must face up to the real possibility that after 200 years of spectacular increases of their material living standards, and of their freedom, the mechanism behind it all — capital formation — is in danger of grinding to a halt. A U.S. Treasury study indicated that total U.S. fixed investment as a percentage of national output during 1960-73 was 17.5 percent.[2] This figure ranks last among a group of 11 major industrial nations. Moreover, the gap between the level of private fixed investment in the U.S., measured as a share of national output, and the investment rates of other industrial nations tended to increase over time.[3] Even Italy and Great Britain, the "sick men" of Europe, have devoted a larger share of output to investment than the United States. Indeed, the most discussed economic issue of the past few years, in board rooms and in academic conclaves, has been the "capital crisis," whereby is meant an emerging capital shortage of awesome proportions. In its well-known study of this subject a few years ago, the New York Stock Exchange projected total capital requirements of the U.S. over a ten-year period — assuming the need to achieve reasonably high levels of employment — at $4.7 trillion. To fund this enormous demand for capital, according to the study, the following savings were anticipated:

	$ (in trillions)
Business depreciation reserves	2.4
Retained earnings	.5
Personal savings of individuals	1.1

for a total of something over $4 trillion. The expected shortfall of required savings came to $650 billion, a staggering sum in any context.[4]

Since the NYSE study was completed, the situation has grown worse. The U.S. personal savings rate is the lowest of any of the major industrial countries. Over the five years 1973-77, Canadians saved 10.3 percent of their disposable personal income, the British 14.1 percent, the West Germans 15.2 percent, the Japanese 24.9 percent, and the Americans only 6.7 percent. That rate has since declined still further, to the 5.1 percent recorded in the last half of 1978. Since personal saving in the U.S. accounts for 65 percent of net private saving, a decline of this magnitude, if it continues, must have a serious impact on capital formation. Meanwhile, savings rates in other industrial nations have risen above their previous high levels in tandem with the increases in the shares of their gross national products allocated to investment. Also, executives and economists alike have been warning that U.S. depreciation schedules are among the lowest in the industrialized world. The schedules currently in effect, it is argued, simply do not permit a sufficiently rapid recovery of capital outlays.

Of course, it is true that in a market economy there is always a shortage of capital in the sense that those who want it would buy more of it if only they could get it at a lower price, or if only the yield from it were larger. There is always a problem of capital insufficiency in the sense that human wants are limitless and everyone wants to better his position if only he could, and there is never enough capital for that purpose. In effect, then, each nation gets the capital formation rate — and thus the rate of employment and the standard of living — it deserves.

The more urgent question is whether the rate "we deserve" — deserve in the sense that our policies brought it about — is consistent with a maximum return for a maximum number of our people on our present wealth, human and non-human. The evidence suggests that we are *not* getting this kind of return, that the productivity of our economy — a function of the ratio of capital to other resources — has been steadily declining and with it the rate of growth of real GNP. As a result, given the long-run growth of our population, our real living standard on a per capita basis is growing only very slowly and may in future be headed downward. In addition, the high secular unemployment which has characterized the American economy, with its disturbing potential for producing political and social disorder, is not likely to decline to any significant degree so long as the capital formation which would have occurred in the absence of certain inhibitions does not in fact occur.

It is these facts, and not just our standing in the international investment league, where national differences make comparisons difficult, which should give us pause. Since 1972, a combination of inflation and taxes has caused the real rate of return for both small and large savers to turn negative. In 1973, the after tax and inflation-adjusted return on accounts in savings and loan associations was around minus 5½ percent. In effect, just as our fisherman friend was harassed by the ruling circles of his world, which inhibited both his wish to save and his will to create capital, our contemporary rulers have raised the risks and reduced the returns of saving. For many, the act of refraining from consumption today in the hope of increased consumption tomorrow is perceived as being merely stupid. Or else savings flee into gold, speculative real estate, old paintings, and the like — dead assets which offer some protection to the saver but do nothing for the enlargement of the economy's capital stock. Indeed, the inflation-induced rise in the value of such assets still further reduces saving since individuals will need to put less aside for retirement and for other future contingencies. The implications of these trends for our future rate of employment and our future economic well-being should be obvious.

BUSINESS SAVINGS IN DECLINE

It is in the business sector, however, that some of the most disturbing elements of the capital crisis are to be found. Consider these facts:

1. Business savings in the U.S., which account for one-third of net private savings, have declined steadily in real terms, that is, after marking up depreciation reserves to offset inflation.

2. Retained earnings, the principal source of business savings, have declined as a percent of gross national product from 13.2 percent in 1960 to 5.6 percent in 1965 to 3.2 percent in 1975, and to less than 3 percent at present. A major contributing factor to this evolution is the high inflation rates that have prevailed since 1972. Embodied in the conventional accounting records of most firms, they have resulted in serious overstatement of real corporate earnings.

3. Non-financial corporations reported profits after taxes in 1974 of $59.7 billion as compared to $37.2 billion in 1965, an impressive 60 percent increase. But when the inflation is taken out of the depreciation reserve, i.e., when current replacement instead of historical cost is used and when the effects of inflation on inventory-values are eliminated, *after tax profits actually declined* by 70 percent from $36.8 billion in 1965 to $10.8 billion in 1974. In effect, they were less than a fifth as large as reported. Because income taxes were payable on a wholly illusory increase in profits, the tax rate on real profits rose from 43 percent in 1965 to 79 percent in 1974, far above the statutory 48 percent ceiling rate on profits established by Congress! 1974 marked, to be sure, the beginning of a recession. Still, by 1976, adjusted after-tax profits were less

than half as large as the reported figure.[5]

Incredibly, in view of these facts, a recent survey conducted by the Opinion Research Corporation showed that a majority of American believe that corporate profits, as a return on stockholders' equity, average 33 percent. The real figure is closer to 5 percent. Small wonder that TV commentators and credulous academics wring their hands over each new surge in *reported* profits. On the other hand, Wall Street was not fooled, nor were stockholders around the country. The word was out: the stock market was a good place to steer clear of.

Since 1968, when the Dow Jones average of industrial stock prices was close to 1,000, the value of the dollar has declined by more than 50 percent, so that in terms of constant dollars — with the Dow Jones average at the end of 1978 at about 700 — the average value of stocks has declined by some 65 percent in ten years. It is thus not surprising that equity financing — the principal alternative to the use of retained profits — has been shrinking. In 1972, underwritings of corporate equities of non-financial businesses amounted to $15.3 billion; in 1973, they were $9.1 billion; and in 1974 only $4.3 billion. In 1977, the equities window opened as loanable funds dried up, and stock offerings rose to $9.9 billion or 25 percent of businesses' total cash requirements. For 1978, however, the stock total fell to $8.8 billion, or less than 9 percent of cash needs. Should this trend continue, U.S. business will perforce turn increasingly to bonds and other forms of borrowing for needed funds. Even now, the equity to debt ratio is $2.43 to $1, dangerously close to the unbalanced debt burden of 1973 and far from the 4 to 1 ratio that characterized the late 1960s.

In effect, the traditional sources of savings for business expansion are tending to dry up — a logical consequence of the exceptionally poor performance of the stock market in the

1970s. Low stock prices have made it unattractive for larger businesses to try to raise money in the equities market and, on the demand side, investors have been slow to buy equities because of the attractive alternatives offered by the huge mountain of debt available at high interest rates.

But the crisis is more profound than the market movements of recent years. The American tax code, much of it conceived in the spirit of soaking the rich for the benefit of the poor, seems deliberately to be aimed at inhibiting savings and capital formation. The bulk of tax revenues in the U.S. come from income taxes, with many of these sharply progressive, rather than from consumption taxes or taxes on production as is the case throughout most of Europe and in Japan. Income taxes are notoriously more damaging to incentives than sales or use taxes, but the United States stubbornly resists moving to a value-added tax, virtually universal in Europe, because it is supposed to be regressive, that is, to fall more heavily on the lower income groups. In fact, we have about reached the limits of our possibilities of squeezing more taxes out of the upper income groups; they are already taxed to the gills, even taking account of so-called "loopholes." It is this fact which, on the one hand, has incited the tax revolt, but on the other pushed the government to even greater reliance on the secret tax of inflation, with all the damage to our economic system that it connotes. Further taxing of the higher income classes can only aggravate the capital shortage, thus jeopardizing existing and future job opportunities for millions of working people.

In the wake of Proposition 13 and the tax revolt that spawned it, it is perhaps safer than it was to assert that the rich are necessary to our system of economy and that a fair degree of income inequality is conducive to economic progress. Both statements are in any case true. For it is the rich who have the means to save. Transferring their incomes in ever larger amounts to lower income groups reduces saving and increases consumption. The needed capital will not be created; job opportunities will dry up; productivity will decline; and inflation will continue.

THE RISING TAX BURDEN

Ironically, in spite of a welter of tax reform measures passed by Congress, the net tax burden on the American people continues to edge up. The 1976 tax law, for example, had a distinctly adverse impact on capital formation. Most of the tax increases embodied in that legislation — applicable to transactions completed before October 31, 1978 — fell on income from capital investments. Thus, it increased the length of time an asset must be held to qualify for the capital gains tax rate, continued the taxation of investment in such vital areas as energy and real estate, increased the marginal tax rate on some incomes previously taxed at a 50 percent rate, and increased the taxable base of inherited capital. In sum, it moved decisively in the direction of promoting more consumption at the expense of investment, steepening the tax system's already pronounced bias against capital formation. A significant reversal of increases in long-term capital gains taxation was achieved in the 1978 federal tax law that followed in the wake of California's Proposition 13 (in the face of determined opposition from the Carter Administration). However, the Kemp-Roth bill, a genuine long-term reform in the direction of lower taxes, went down to defeat. Moreover, U.S. tax policy continues to permit businesses to deduct interest payments on debt, but not on dividend payments on stock, perpetuating the historic distortion in the supply of and demand for capital embodied in such double taxation. And though, as noted, capital gains taxes have come down measurably, a great deal of uncertainty surrounds the future of such taxation and the direction it will take.

President Carter's difficulties in trying to pare a federal budget swollen by subsidies and transfers to hundreds of entrenched special interests shows that the Congress has not yet fully grasped these facts: that the American economy has been taxed to its feasible limits; that increasing the tax take is likely to shrink the tax base itself because of diminished output; that even the total expropriation of all incomes over $100,000 would make only a negligible addition, percentage-wise, to total tax revenues; that the great bulk of taxable income is produced by the middle class; that the great bulk of taxable income is produced by the middle class; that it is this class which receives the great bulk of government services, and that it will have to pay for them; that there is no "fourth dimension" of potential revenues waiting out there to be garnered. The advent of Howard Jarvis, Proposition 13, and calls for a constitutional convention to prohibit deficit spending, show that the great middle class of citizens is awakening to these truths. This class appears now to recognize, indeed, that it is no longer a question of the government's robbing Peter to pay Paul, but of robbing Peter to pay Peter.

But the hour is late and the momentum in the other direction is formidable. Two dimensions of this trend — the one the product of the furious egalitarianism of recent years and the other the product of a deep-seated hostility to business and the market economy — deserve comment. These are, first, on the quantitative side, the spectacular increase in government transfer payments and second, on the qualitative side, the exponentially expanding maze of government regulations, directives, prescriptions and controls imposed on the private sector.

The social spending of the U.S. in the past 25 years has literally exploded. Since 1950, social welfare expenditures have risen from $24 billion to some $283 billion (FY 1980). The number of persons on welfare, excluding the elderly and disabled, now hovers at around 12 million persons. More than twenty million persons receive food stamps. Transfer payments — which are moneys taken from income producers and given to non-producers in the framework of such programs as Social Security, Medicare, unemployment compensation, public assistance, etc. — increased from 20 percent of total Federal expenditures in 1950 to well over 50 percent in 1978. Without making a value judgment on whether the programs in question are necessary or unnecessary, or are too big or too small, it is evident that money that might have been saved and made available for capital formation and transferred to non-producers resulting in an increase in consumption and a reduction in the economy's job-creating potential.

THE IMPACT OF THE SOCIAL SECURITY SYSTEM

The growing consumption bias in the economy is especially evident in the Social Security system, a nominal insurance scheme which, however, is funded not from a previously saved reserve, which would have been available for investment, but from current tax payments of working people. Because of continuing legally mandated increases in benefits, aggravated by an inflation escalation factor, beyond current and prospective receipts, the unfunded liabilities of the system have grown horrendously to somewhere between $2.5 and $3 trillion. Moreover, the system, once conceived of as merely a floor under private pension programs, has expanded in its coverages and benefits to the point where for a majority of Americans, anticipated Social Security benefits are the most important form of family wealth. It is obvious that the effect of this must be to reduce the need to build up private reserves against the contingencies of old age and thus to reduce private saving. An expert on the economic impact of the Social Security system, Dr. Martin Feldstein of Harvard, concluded from data developed for 1971 that Social Security taxes in that year reduced private saving by $61 billion.[6] Since actual personal saving for the year amounted also to $61 billion, the apparent effect of the Social Security system was to reduce private saving by half. In light of the shrinkage of business saving described earlier, the gravity of this kind of contraction of private saving — the remaining source of funds for capital formation — needs no emphasis. In its present form, the Social Security system, while increasing consumption, hampers the economy's ability to increase output and to create jobs, thus contributing to the twin evils of inflation and stagnation.

All government transfers tend to shift wealth from individuals with a positive marginal propensity to save to individuals with predictably lower or zero saving rates. The ineluctable result is *less total saving.* Moreover, to the degree that government finances its growing spending, for all purposes, through the issuance of government securities rather than by taxes, it competes directly with the private sector for the available real capital. Government budget deficits are bound in some degree to "crowd out" private borrowers from the capital markets, thus inhibiting increases in the economy's productive capacity needed to keep pace with the growing labor force.

GOVERNMENT REGULATION: GROWING IMPEDIMENT TO JOB CREATION

While rising levels of taxation and continuous federal budget deficits have been major contributions to unemployment and inflation for almost two decades, another government-created obstacle to economic progress has assumed especial importance recently: the pervasive and still expanding interventions of government in the economy via its rules, regulations, controls, restrictions, and overriding of private rights, whether enacted by Congress or imposed by fiat of the courts or quasi-judicial government agencies (of which the number is still growing in spite of a plethora of rhetoric about government simplification and reorganization). A great number of these interventions have significantly raised the costs and risks of investment while reducing its yield. Examples include price controls in a variety of areas and notably in oil, natural gas, and residential real estate (rent controls), with a return to generalized wage and price controls a distinct possibility. From agencies such as the Occupational Safety and Health Administration (OSHA), the Environmental Protection Agency (EPA), the Federal Energy Administration (FEA), the Interstate Commerce Commission (ICC), and many others, issues a daily flood of directives specifying what businesses can or cannot do. This process, kept in motion by zealous bureaucrats, must lead in the end to economic strangulation.

While the excesses of the agencies mentioned do not mean that the government does not have a positive and constructive regulatory role to play, the sheer mass of regulations now on the books threatens to overwhelm the private sector. Many of these are issued capriciously, are confused or ambiguous, and are often at cross purposes with previously issued regulations of sister agencies. Though some efforts at de-regulation have been successful, for example, the gradual dismantlement of the Civil Aeronautics Board (CAB), the likelihood is high that the regulatory tide will continue to rise. The resulting uncertainties will tend to eliminate marginal · investments because of the increased risk. For a businessman to be required to show that a new product does *not* tend to cause a variety of detrimental side effects may be as costly as the development of the new product itself. Uncertainty — the foreknowledge that government is likely to change the rules — diminishes the confidence of investors and entrepreneurs in all the existing rules. The present value of a piece of capital is in this fashion reduced because the uncertainty of its value tomorrow has been increased.

The Dow Chemical Company fiasco in California is a case in point. In 1975, Dow announced plans to build a $500 million petrochemical complex on the Sacramento River. But in January 1977, after spending $10 million on land and planning, the Company abandoned the project. It did so because in two years it had succeeded in obtaining only four of the 65 permits required from twelve local, state, and federal agencies to begin construction. The cost? Some 1,200 construction jobs, 1,000 permanent jobs, and a $15 million annual payroll at a time when California's unemployment rate was over 9 percent.

In the end, the spectre of chronically inadequate capital formation, and the chronic unemployment that attends it, will continue to haunt the American economy as long as the government policies that created the spectre are not changed. Foremost among these policies is toleration of inflation, closely followed by punitive taxation and over-regulation. The question of moment is whether the processes that have been set in motion over the past 40 years under the rubric of the welfare state can be reversed or even halted. History is littered with the wrecks of cultures that have foundered under the weight of too much government.

Above all it is the great inflation of the 1970s that has eaten away at the very vitals of the American economy, rewarded the powerful and punished the weak, perverted all market processes, and distorted the role of profits, prices and wages. Inevitably, it has also transformed boom into bust. Inflation gone amuck always produces depression and unemployment and it did so in the great downturn of 1973-75, with its immense costs in economic and human terms. At bottom, of course, inflation is not an economic phenomenon only, but a symptom of a process of moral rot at work in the body politic, and it requires a moral response from those who are its short-term beneficiaries and ultimate victims. Do we have the guts to finally repeal those laws of the welfare state that result in the manufacture of money for non-existent goods, those powers of labor unions that raise pay in excess of productivity, and those acts and regulations of government, as well as of private firms, that impede competition, distort the allocation of resources, diminish savings, punish entrepreneurship and otherwise vitiate the functioning of our market economy?

Whether the menace of inflation — and its associated evils of a constantly shrinking capital base and rising unemployment — can be dispelled depends on the answers that are made to these fundamental questions.

FOOTNOTES

1. Cf. Bauer, P.T., *Dissent on Development: Studies and Debates in Development Economics*, Harvard University Press, Cambridge, Mass., 1972.
2. U.S. Treasury, *Treasury Papers*, April 1976, Washington, D.C.
3. *Business Week*, "The U.S. Bias Against Saving," December 11, 1978, p. 93.
4. O'Brien, E. I., "Capital Formation," *Vital Speeches of the Day*, September 15, 1975, pp. 728 ff.
5. Terborgh, George, "Inflation and Profits," *Memorandum*, Machinery & Allied Products Institute, Washington, D.C., October 1976.
6. Cf. Feldstein, Martin, "Facing the Social Security Crisis," *The Public Interest*, New York, Spring 1977, pp. 88 ff.

IX

UNEMPLOYMENT, WELFARE AND ECONOMIC GROWTH

Steven D. Symms

Unemployment is one of the great problems of our time, although it is no longer the major cause of poverty in the United States, due to the vast welfare system which has been developed during the past forty years. But while relieving poverty, the welfare system itself has become one of the nation's major problems.

The American people are among the most charitable in the world, and prior to the great depression private charity helped to alleviate much — or, as some people will argue, at least some — of the abject poverty resulting from unemployment, old age and disabilities. As a result of the growing urbanization, however, which weakened and destroyed personal contacts between neighbors, and the devastating effects of the great depression, private charity became inadequate to meet modern welfare concepts and has now largely been replaced by public welfare, financed by taxes rather than the desire of the people to help their less fortunate neighbors. In fact the very word "charity" has acquired a demeaning connotation. Those in need now have a "right" to be supported by society, and what constitutes "need" — the "poverty level" in modern parlance — is being determined by politicians who are anxious to buy the votes of the "needy," and by the bureaucracy which steadily expands by catering to the "needy" and by discovering more "needy." All this is at the expense of the taxpayer, the growth of the economy, and the stability of the dollar, which is undermined to the extent that the welfare bill is paid with the help of the printing press.

That the present welfare system is incredibly inefficient and enormously expensive is becoming increasingly clear to more and more millions of Americans. But it is less obvious to many that the welfare mess is to a large extent the result of the nation's — or the government's — failure to cope with the unemployment problem. The two popular notions that it is the fault of "society" that millions of men, women and teenagers cannot find work — or at least the type of work they want — and that it is hence the duty of "society" to support the "needy" through welfare have been linked into one inseparable socio-economic philosophy, which, in the end, can destroy the economic basis of the country and the texture of our society.

To the extent that the welfare system increases the inflationary pressure — and there is little doubt that it does — it constitutes the cruelest tax of all on the elderly and those forced to live on a fixed income.

The professional problem-solvers continue to draw their hefty salaries, while vast amounts of the assistance continues to go to those for whom it was never originally intended.

The reason for all this is clear and cannot be separated from any federal system we devise. It is a simple fact that a federal employee wants not only to do a good job, but wants to expand it. Those who work in welfare have a natural incentive

to add people to their rolls and a natural desire to show their superiors how badly their programs are needed. Just as the private businessman wants to increase his business, so do the federal bureaucrats have the natural desire to expand their agencies and to seek promotion. The net result is to encourage more people to come into the programs and to avoid putting people out of the programs.
out of the programs.

In addition, a person who is on welfare but doesn't need it will rarely complain whereas the person who is taken off or refused will usually raise a loud cry of protest. It is only human nature to attempt to avoid the complaints and to give your superiors the appearance that everyone is happy with your work.

No one, therefore, should be surprised that there is a vast amount of fraud and abuse in the system. As long as it is administered by federal agencies and federal employees, there is no realistic way to clean it up.

WELFARE FRAUDS

At one point, more than 40 percent of the cases in the Aid to Families with Dependent Children involved wrongful payments. That is inefficiency and that is only one of several welfare programs. The Department of Health, Education and Welfare has issued so-called tolerance levels of 3 percent fraud and 5 percent overpayment. Aside from the fact that this 8 percent allows a $5 billion leeway for abuse and inefficiency, HEW has only 10 inspectors to deal with a ten-year backlog of fraud cases. They have an impossible job.

Abuse abounds in the system. Official documentation in Pennsylvania attests that food stamps have been used for the purchase of items from liquor to shotguns and even in payment for prostitution.

Illinois has documented frauds including a case where an employed women, who had won a $10,000 lottery, was collecting welfare; and another case in which the wife claimed her husband had deserted the family 10 years ago so she was drawing welfare, yet her husband had a joint checking account and both were signing checks regularly. They had also recently co-signed for a $10,000 Small Business Administration loan and had jointly purchased a fish market.

Another documented example in Massachusetts involved a woman, notoriously known as the "welfare queen," who drew cash payments, food stamps, medical treatment and other services equal to a $20,000 income. While these specific cases have received wide publicity because of their outrageous nature, the multitude of less flagrant abuses remain undiscovered and continue. Clearly, inefficiency does foster fraud and it is important that Congress recognize just how serious this problem has become.

THE COST OF WELFARE AND CAPITAL FORMATION

The enormous expense of the welfare system borne by the American taxpayers is, however, a far more serious problem than its abuses. Even if we assume that the cost would decrease with greater efficiency, the costs are already far too high, and continue to grow.

The plain hard economic fact is that every time a dollar is taxed out of the private sector to be redistributed to someone in need, the ability of the private sector to generate the capital necessary to create new jobs is reduced. Government has grown at the expense of private investment and development, and the net result of a welfare program which has become too large is a loss of the ability in the private sector to supply the goods and services necessary for a good standard of living. In other words, welfare programs that were designed originally with the high and good purpose of reducing poverty may in the end cause more poverty than they prevent.

Most people today are beginning to realize that something terribly serious is happening to the economy of our country. The value of the dollar is shrinking, the quality of goods is decreasing as companies "cut corners" in order to hold down prices, farm income is dropping to the point that many farmers are no longer able to make enough to meet their costs of production, and millions of people on fixed incomes are becoming desperate as they find that pension checks will not buy proper food, heat and clothing and in some cases will not even pay the property tax on homes which are bought and paid for.

The problem is simply that welfare costs are eroding the nation's ability to produce, and since the costs of the programs exceed government income, they are paid for with newly printed money, thus fueling the fires of inflation.

In 1970 the costs of welfare were approximately $20 billion, in 1972 about $30 billion and in 1977 around $60 billion and they continue to increase. At the current rate of increase, welfare cost would reach approximately $450 billion in twelve years! Of course long before reaching that figure the nation will have a monetary crisis of such severe proportions that government as we know it will no longer be functioning.

ADMINISTRATIVE COST AND THE POLITICAL CAUSES

The cost of administering these programs is also increasing as more people must be added to the government payroll to manage the programs. A fair estimate is that about 300,000 people are now on state or federal payrolls to administer welfare programs. Agriculture Secretary Bob Bergland stated on March 10, 1977, that the administrative costs of the Food Stamp program alone exceeded $600,000 per day.

In addition to the cost that the taxpayer must bear, no one can calculate the loss to the total economy which is represented by taking 300,000 workers out of production and putting them into government administration.

The problem we face is mammoth and is growing daily. Whether these problems will receive attention is up to the Congressional leadershop. The Democrats at this writing are in firm control of the Congress and have a two-to-one majority. The Democratic President could push for consideration of major reforms and Congress could easily pass any program changes which he suggested. But, the truth of the matter is that the majority is controlled by the liberals, and the liberals have no intention of solving the problem by reducing the welfare load. The liberal constituency in this country is made up of a majority of non-producers. It is therefore in their political interest to continue heavy spending on government handouts.

Reality dictates that the only viable solution is to unseat the liberals and elect conservatives. To end the needless drain on our tax dollars we must have a majority in Congress that believes in freedom and owes its first loyalty to the hard-working middle class taxpayer. Unless this happens the takers will continue to increase their dependence on the producers until the producers are no longer able to carry the load and the economy becomes so weak that most Americans will be living in poverty.

SUGGESTED SOLUTIONS

What then should be done?

First of all, serious attempts must be made to limit the escalation of costs, the outright fraud and the cheating. Good legislation aimed at this goal will have some chance of passing even in a liberal Congress.

Certainly we should be able to ask that people requesting welfare register for work, and be willing to accept jobs which are available in the community, even if these jobs are not as desirable as they might wish, and even if the salaries paid on those jobs are less than the welfare benefits which the person is currently receiving. It is obviously difficult to make people work in low-paid jobs if they are making almost as much, or even more, by remaining on welfare.

Much greater emphasis must be placed on quality control. Requirements for food stamps should be tightened and stiffer penalties for fraud enforced.

WELFARE NOT THE SOLUTION

However, welfare reform alone is not going to be a realistic long-term solution because welfare itself is the wrong method of solving a problem which is being fundamentally misunderstood.

The goal which we all seek, liberals and conservatives alike, is a higher standard of living for all, and freedom and dignity for every American.

Federal welfare programs because of their very nature tend over a long period of time to have just the opposite effect. There are of course some people who because of physical or mental disabilities must be cared for by their more fortunate fellow citizens, but the vast bulk of welfare is aimed at people who because of social or economic causes are unable to earn enough to have a reasonable standard of living.

There are many reasons for this inability to earn a reasonable living. In some areas there are simply not enough jobs available. In other instances there are jobs but those jobs require skills which are not possessed by the people applying for them. In still other cases there are jobs but the pay scales are too low to support people even if they do work. Sometimes a mother finds herself with small children who would receive no care if she left the home. And there are many other reasons.

How can we solve this problem? The answer it seems to me is obvious. It will disappear if there is a rising standard of living, accompanied by an economic situation where there are more high-paying jobs than there are people to fill those jobs. Also there must be enough information and freedom to move about so that people and jobs are brought together.

Having said that, however, we must recognize that achieving the solution is not simple and it is not easy. In order to create a society with a rising standard of living, with more jobs than there are people, and with adequate information and mobility, government must exercise an enormous amount of skill, restraint and commitment to long-term goals.

There is enough information now available to create such a society. The knowledge available from history, from contemporary government experiments around the world, from psychology and from our own experiences here in America is more than adequate to shape this kind of productive society.

Briefly, the solution to poverty and all the hardship which goes with it must come from a rededication to the principles laid down for this nation by the men who founded it. They knew that the most dynamic force in the world was the creativity and energy of free men who were able to own their own property, manage their own affairs and keep what they earned. They tried to set up a government so structured that liberty was protected not only from the edicts of the powerful, but also from the whims of the majority; under it men could dream dreams, create new products and build a world of virtually unlimited prosperity.

History has proved them correct, and America has already done more to find real answers to poverty and misery than any other nation at any time on the face of the earth.

These principles have not changed and as society becomes more and more complex, it becomes increasingly important to apply them. Socialism and centralized control may work to a certain extent in a backward and simple society. It cannot work effectively in a highly complex technical society. As our world becomes more technical, it becomes increasingly impossible for any centralized agency or any individual to possess enough knowledge to make intelligent decisions about research, production and marketing for the whole country. These decisions to be accurate must be made by individuals who are highly trained and who are in constant contact with the technical information required.

If every decision must be approved by a government agency before it can be put into effect, the time required to educate the government becomes so great that progress is slowed to totally unacceptable levels. In addition, enough money must be retained in the private sector for capital investment to allow a steady improvement in our ability to produce more quality goods at steadily lower costs.

This nation is now in a position to have a society where poverty and sickness can be largely eliminated. We have a high technology. We have the most skilled work force which has ever existed and we have a virtually unlimited supply of energy if the government would get out of the way and allow it to be developed and used.

In spite of the billions being spent for so-called "people" programs, the people involved are finding that conditions are growing worse instead of better. The cities are bankrupt. Life in the ghettos is growing worse. Business is in trouble and most people recognize that the whole U.S. economy is headed for a serious crisis unless major changes are made in our energy and capital investment policies.

However, in order to effectively explain this message, it

is important for conservatives to do at least two things which they are not doing now. First of all, they must stop talking to themselves and start selling their message to the country at large, expecially the liberals.

A good example of this recently occurred in Idaho. A friend of mine, Ralph Smeed, sometimes referred to as the "Idaho Conservative Libertarian Guru" made friends with a very liberal editor of one of the major newspapers. Over a period of time that editor has become a well-informed and very conservative libertarian writer.

The point is simple. To win the conservative battle requires education and patience. The facts are on our side and with patience we can win the battle.

The second thing that conservatives must do is to explain to people and to the media that our point of view is the most humanitarian view of all.

All of history and all human experience show that government is the major source of oppression and cruelty and that freedom is one of mankind's most precious possessions.

We conservatives are the ones who are fighting oppressions and poverty and working for freedom and prosperity. The people with the welfare mentality are the ones who will in the long run destroy freedom and reduce this country to a place where poverty is common.

We can and should have a great future in this country. We must get rid of the pessimists and the politicians who would rather have personal power for themselves at the expense of the average American citizen. If we can turn the American producer loose and set him free from too much taxation, excessive regulation and massive inflation, we can have a society where living standards will steadily rise, where there are more jobs than there are people for those jobs, and where there is enough information and personal mobility for people to find and fill those jobs.

Welfare has become so large and so destructive to the private sector that immediate and massive reform is necessary. However, the goal toward which we should all work is a society which because of individual liberty and creativity becomes so prosperous that welfare from government at any level is no longer necessary.

X

ABOLISH THE GOLD STANDARD AND PRIME THE PUMP

Donald L. Kemmerer

In 1912, there were 41 nations on the gold standard including nearly all the major nations of the world. The gold standard is a monetary system in which the measuring unit of value, say the dollar, is a certain weight of gold. Thus the dollar was what that amount of gold would buy. All paper dollars and even checking accounts were convertible into gold dollars on demand. Prior to World War I nations that had inconvertible currencies or chronically unbalanced budgets were regarded as either backward or irresponsible.

The late Dr. Melchior Palyi wrote in his *Twilight of Gold*, "The gold standard was 'sacrosanct' to the generations brought up on the Adam Smith ideals of free markets ... it was an essential instrument of economic freedom. It protected the individual against arbitrary measures of the government by offering a convenient hedge against . . . the depreciation or devaluation of the currency. Above all, it raised a mighty barrier against authoritarian interference with the economic process." Palyi quoted Sir Roy Harrod that opposing the gold standard before World War I "was confined to cranks and very few academic economists. Its . . . desirability was not a live issue." Harrod is Lord J. M. Keynes biographer and himself no friend of the gold standard. The gold standard's development and widespread adoption after the 1870's was regarded as one of the great advances in the realm of the social sciences in modern times, and Great Britain's management of the gold standard (gold coin variety) with very modest reserves was admired by central bankers all over the world.

As for unemployment, it was not the major or even the foremost economic issue that it has been starting with the Great Depression. Although not ignored, little if any public effort was made to relieve it. Any economist who contended that expanding the money supply was a good way to reduce unemployment was certain to receive sharp criticism from his colleagues. The quality of the unemployment statistics then available is perhaps the best measure of the importance of that issue. They were not looked upon as very reliable.

The shock of World War I (1914-18) sooner or later drove every nation off the gold standard. The war and its aftermath also produced the worst inflation (in Germany, Austria, Hungary, Poland and Russia) the world had seen since the French Revolution. The buying power of the monetary units of even the victorious nations dropped by 60 percent to 90 percent and by the early 1920's three things had happened.

1) International monetary conventions at Brussels in 1920 and at Genoa in 1922 both strongly affirmed the desire of all participating nations to return to the discipline and security of the gold standard "as soon as possible." The United States had already returned on June 10, 1919. During the 1920's a veritable parade of nations went back on gold, a total of 50 by 1931.

2) Because the inflations had so increased the money

supply, and the costs of war had sent so much of the world's gold to the United States, there no longer seemed to be enough gold available for so many nations to be on the gold *coin* standard. Countries adopted more economical forms of the system. Britain devised the gold bullion standard under which the only gold "coins" into which her paper pounds were redeemable were gold ingots worth about $8,300 each. They rarely circulated. Many lesser nations adopted an even more economical form, the gold exchange standard, under which they kept a bank account with a gold bullion or gold coin standard nation and had their currencies redeemable in that nation's currency. This system was abused with disastrous results.

3) The World War I experience convinced high government officials that the objections of the "high priests" of central banks, i.e., their managers, to easy credit expansion and to other financial "taboos" of pre-war days could be ignored without courting immediate disaster, or, as some believed, any foreseeable disaster at all. To change the metaphor, once these finance ministers had seen the "Gay Paree" of easy money practices, it was hard to get them back again "on the farm" of sound monetary policies.

The United States price levels were remarkably stable during most of the 1920's from 1922 to '30 which suggests that its gold standard was performing reasonably well.

Yet, paradoxically there was mounting dissatisfaction with it among some economists. On the one hand, followers of Britain's John Maynard Keynes found it was too restrictive of government monetary policy. On the other hand, disciples of Yale's Irving Fisher contended that in the past the gold standard had not provided a sufficiently stable price level. Fisher liked to point to a 72 percent drop in the buying power of the dollar between 1896 and 1920. Both groups had support from a third quarter, led by Sweden's Gustav Cassel, who complained that there was no longer enough gold: the supply was increasing more slowly than the needs of the world's economies, with deflation a certain consequence.

THE GREAT DEPRESSION

In 1929 the Great Depression began in the United States, ushered in by the stock market crash of October, 1929. That was the first jab of a one-to-three series of blows that sent the American economy and others in the Western world reeling from the shock.

The second was in the summer of 1931 when in rapid succession Austria, Germany and Great Britain abandoned their gold standards. Britain's most cited explanation was that she had returned to gold prematurely in May of 1925, or else at too high a rate for the pound, and therefore could not lower wages, hence prices, enough to compete satisfactorily in world trade. She made the gold standard the scapegoat with Keynes and others attacking gold as a "relic of barbarism." Britain's departure from gold also swept off all her satellites whose gold exchange standards were tied to the pound sterling. The indirect after-effects were still felt months later. In the summer of 1932, according to President Herbert Hoover, even the United States gold standard was in danger because of heavy gold outflows.

The third blow was the collapse of the American banking system in early 1933. It had been crumbling for some time. In the five years, 1929-33 9,765 banks closed, culminating in the "Bank Holiday" of early March 1933.

There seemed to be no end to the long depressions with its tens of thousands of business failures of all kinds and its dreary lines of hungry, discouraged people in every large city waiting for hand-outs at local soup kitchens. There were said to be 12 to 16 millions of unemployed — no one was sure what the right figure was — a quarter to a third of the nation's working force.

At all such times there appear many persons proposing remedies to relieve the "hard times." Some of these individuals simply want to be helpful, some are seeking the limelight, and a fair number are power grabbers. "Money cranks" are especially numerous and their nostrums notably dubious, for few people truly understand money. In the early 1930's the more widely discussed diagnoses grew out of the complaints and analyses previously aired, mostly among intellectuals. Much of the monetary legislation in this 1933-35 era can be traced to the criticisms of the gold standard just mentioned.

Followers of Keynes were pleased to see the gold standard abandoned in England in 1931, briefly in the United States in 1933, everywhere else but in the United States by 1936, and a watered down version adopted in the United States when it came back to gold in January, 1934. Admirers of Irving Fisher, among them Professor George Warren of Cornell, felt that a first step had been taken in adopting Fisher's complex idea of a non-circulating gold dollar whose varying weight would presumably keep the price level more stable. And disciples of Gustav Cassel could be pleased to see the allegedly deflationary gold standard abandoned except in the United States and even there the gold content of the dollar was reduced thus making the gold go farther. The only really unhappy economists were those who believed that the gold standard, despite its faults, more than normally manifest at the time, was still the best monetary system fallible man had ever developed. In 1933 they formed an organization called the Economists National Committee on Monetary Policy with Professor Ray Westerfield of Yale its first president, Professor Walter E. Spahr of N.Y.U. its secretary, and most of the leading monetary experts of that time as members. This organization is in many ways the father of C.M.R.E.

Yet compromising differences between distinguished professors was not the motive for these revolutionary money developments, and more were to come. The president, senators and congressmen and other government officials had to believe it would improve the economic situation, please various segments of their constituencies, bring them fame as benefactors and enhance their political power. But even they did not agree on how to achieve these goals except in one respect — the money supply would have to be increased. This agreement was most visible in the Thomas Amendment of May 12, 1933 to the Agricultural Adjustment Act (the AAA). This Amendment gave President Franklin D. Roosevelt power, at his discretion, to take any or all of the following steps: (1) to devalue the dollar by as much as 50 per cent; (2) to issue $3 billions of greenbacks; (3) to put the nation on a bimetallic standard (shades of William Jennings Bryan), and (4) to engage in $3 billions of Federal Reserve open market buying operations (the equivalent then, over time, of increasing the money supply by $30 billions). Congress was much more reckless than the President! Roosevelt used only part of one of these powers — he devalued the dollar by 41% the following year — which was bad enough, although clearly he could have taken far greater inflationary strides. Congress finally removed this "sword of Damocles" — like the Thomas Amendment, piece by piece, between 1943 and 1945.

And why was there such widespread agreement that the government should increase the money supply?

To start with, the price level had dropped sharply from the stable levels of the 1920's — down, in fact, to the 1913 or pre-war level. By February 1933 wholesale prices had fallen 41 per cent from the base or so-called normal year of the 1920's, 1926. In the memory of men, then, depressions had always been characterized by deflation. Great prosperity, too, can produce deflation — the 1880's in this country saw phenomenal industrial growth and deflation — but that is another story. To the simple-minded, and even to many who were not so simple-minded, the logic of the situation called for an increase in the price level by means of an increase in the money supply. When prices were back to the level that they associated with prosperity, it would bring back prosperity. Wiser heads said that made as much sense as a doctor giving his feverish patient ice cubes to suck before taking his temperature to get the patient's temperature down. Various ways of increasing the price level were proposed — that is why the Thomas amendment was truly "a mixed bag." Notice that even the Far Western states, where silver was such an important by-product of their mining industry, got a return to bimetallism included as one of the choices.

THE PRIMING OF THE PUMP

There was another much publicized rationale for increasing the money supply. That was the underconsumption theory. It had been around for a long time but had not enjoyed much respect until the latter 1920's, the 1930's and since. In this country an economist and president of the Pollak Foundation for Economic Research, William T. Foster, and a manufacturer and investment banker, Waddill Catchings, wrote several books together between 1925 and 1927, in which they stressed the importance of putting enough money, i.e., buying power, in the hands of the people to maintain prosperity. Marriner Eccles, Utah banker and destined to be chairman of the board of governors of the Federal Reserve System from 1936 to 1948 was a disciple of Foster and Catchings. Columbia University's Rexford Guy Tugwell, economist, planner and "brain trust" advisor to President Franklin D. Roosevelt, had similar beliefs. Meanwhile in England a more renowned economist, Professor

John Maynard Keynes, of Cambridge University, was reaching similar conclusions and writing a book setting forth his ideas of how to relieve unemployment and restore prosperity and maintain it. That book, *The General Theory*, would profoundly affect economic thinking and governmental financial policies for at least the next two generations. Put in very simple terms he was saying that it was vital for the public to have the purchasing power to buy goods to get the wheels of industry moving again. When industries themselves could not hire the people and thus provide them with the purchasing power, then government should step in.

Plans were soon underway to pay indigent hundreds of thousands to rake leaves, dig holes, do almost anything plausibly useful — these activities came to be called "boondoggles" — to earn that purchasing power. This was the Works Progress Administration, or WPA. And there were other more defensible spending programs such as the Civilian Conservation Corps and the Public Works Administration. All of these, but the make-shift WPA in particular, had as their goal to put purchasing power in the hands of the masses, restore the flow of money to industry, and in time make the private sector self-sufficient again. This was called "priming the pump." In the days of well pumps on farms, when the pump went dry and suction would not bring water up the pump pipe, the common way of remedying the situation was to pour some water down the pump pipe thus wetting and expanding the suction device at the bottom and restoring its ability to bring water up. A little water poured down would, with the aid of pumping, start the return flow of much more water.

This new "liberal" remedy differs from the older conservative belief that man must first produce goods and sell them for what he can, for only that will start the economy functioning again in a healthy way. New Deal economists argued that the recipients of wages for these "boondoggles" and low priority public projects would promptly spend that income for food, clothing, furniture and other items, thus stimulating the industries producing those goods. Conservative economists tended to believe that just placing the emphasis on "putting money into circulation" would result in shoddy or unneeded production, false expectations on the part of the people thus employed and price inflation in the long run and would not really solve the unemployment problem. A few conservatives went so far as to say that every time a dollar changes hands, the world is poorer if the payer does not receive a valued product or service in return.

In summary, two actions, allegedly, would reduce unemployment and restore prosperity. One was increasing the money supply and thereby raising the price level. The other was putting more money into the hands of the people and thus "priming the pump."

We are now back again to how *actually* the New Deal increased the money supply, by money is meant not only currency (coins and bills) but also checking accounts, generally called demand deposits. Of the two, checking accounts were then about seven times as great as the currency. The expansion of both, however, was limited by the gold legal reserve requirement. Three main steps were taken in the 1930's to increase the money supply and get it into the hands of the people.

1) Under President Hoover, in 1932, Congress temporarily authorized Federal Reserve Banks to use government bonds as secondary reserves. This is one of the least understood yet most far-reaching banking laws Congress ever enacted. prior to this, certain types of promissory notes and drafts or gold itself were required. The 1932 law was later made permanent. It opened the way for monetizing the public debt, the tap root of American inflationary troubles over the past generation. It has, however, done more damage to our economy since the

1940's than it did in the 1930's.

2) To solve the supposed shortage of gold problem President Roosevelt did four major things during his first year in office. (A) In March of 1933 he had the Treasury confiscate just about all American gold coins. That suggests that he already had devaluation in mind. (B) He had Congress, by Joint Resolution of both houses on June 5, 1933 declare the gold clause in all contracts no longer enforceable. (C) Starting in August he had the Treasury start bidding up the price of newly mined gold. (D) On January 30, 1934 he set the new price of gold at $35 a troy ounce. For most of the previous century it had been at $20.67 a troy ounce.

To say that the government "set" the price of gold at $20.67 an ounce or at $35 an ounce creates a false impression. So long as the government mints gold coins, they must be of uniform size, that is, have the same number of grains of gold per dollar. Before 1934 the gold dollar had 23.22 grains of pure gold per dollar. Thus from every troy ounce of gold, 480 grains, the Mint could coin $20.67. 23.22 goes into 480 20.67 times. That was called the "mint price." In January, 1934 it reduced the number of grains of gold per dollar to 13.71. Now the mint could coin $35 out of each troy ounce. 13.71 goes into 480 exactly 35 times.

The 1933-1934 American devaluation was unique: It is the only one caused by deflation (not inflation) and intended to bring about *higher* prices, not stable prices. It did raise them eventually but not immediately, as hoped.

Why did the government choose this 13.71 grain figure? In February, 1933, just before Roosevelt took office on March 4 the wholesale price index was 41 percent below the alleged 1926 norm. Roosevelt's close friend and second Secretary of the Treasury, Henry Morgenthau Jr., was himself a friend and former student of George Warren, Professor of Agricultural Economics at Cornell University, and had recommended

Warren and his ideas on how to raise the price level to President Roosevelt. Warren said that if you reduced the gold content of the dollar by one half, it would cause prices to double — two being the reciprocal of one half. It followed that to get prices which had declined by 41 percent since 1926 back up to that 1926 level, you cut the size of the dollar by 41 percent which would cause prices to rise 69 percent — 1.69 is the reciprocal of .41. Almost presto, prices would go back to the desired 1926 level. Or so at least Professor Warren reasoned.

The chief price that went up presto was the mint price of gold. That so stimulated gold mining everywhere that within three years American gold holdings had risen by two thirds and there was fear of another speculative boom like that ending in 1929. A moderate one did take place in 1936-37. Prices of imported goods also tended immediately to rise by two thirds. But consumer and wholesale price (BLS indices), to the intense disappointment of George Warren and his fellow believers, rose respectively by only about 7 and 15 percent over the three years, 1934-37. But over a longer period this unnecessary devaluation gave the nation a strong push down the inflationary road it has been travelling ever since.

3) Although federal government revenues averaged $4 billions more or less a year during the 1930's — incredibly modest compared to today's magnitudes — the expenditures ran about two-thirds higher than that figure. For the time those were substantial deficits. Very roughly a third of those expenditures went to support the various programs created to relieve the unemployment situation, to put "purchasing power" in the hands of the people. They looked like the considerate act of a benevolent government and no doubt were on the part of many officials. If these outlays had reduced the unemployment and restored prosperity, as the economist disciples of Keynes and of Foster and Catchings thought they

would, this spending cost not have been seriously criticized.

But was benevolence the chief motive of these manipulations of the money supply and these billions of dollars of outlays? President Roosevelt's perennial advisor and sometime cabinet member boasted in 1940 that the administration's goal was "to tax and tax, spend and spend, elect and elect." A gold standard under which not only foreign governments and central banks but also American citizens could have demanded gold coin — the kind of gold standard the United States had before 1933 — would have given those who questioned Washington's politics, or doubted its efficacy, an opportunity to express their doubts by demanding gold coins and to protect themselves against future loss of capital.

Did these enormous expenditures relieve the unemployment situation? The gathering and processing of unemployment statistics improved a little during the 1930's. If we accept the new official Bureau of Labor Statistics figures for 1933 and 1939 as the best available, 12.8 millions and 9.5 millions respectively, we see that a terrific amount of governmental planning and expenditure had produced only a modest improvement. The 1939 figure represented a 17 percent rate of unemployed by today's standards! Never before in American history had the nation spent so much to relieve a depression and never had the depression and accompanying unemployment lasted so long.

This experience should have taught Americans a lesson, that spending lavishly to put purchasing power in the hands of the people is not a satisfactory way to reduce unemployment. But did it? As the old saying goes, "Those who will not remember history are doomed to repeat it." And this time on a much grander scale.

XI

UNEMPLOYMENT AND INFLATION IN MEXICO

Agustin Navarro Gergely

The essays in this book deal primarily with the problem of unemployment in the United States. Conditions are far more critical in Mexico, and, at first sight, there seems no justification for drawing parallels — even by implication — between the politico-economic conditions of the two countries. The economic and technological resources of the United States are very much larger than those of Mexico, and the U.S., as a whole, has a far stronger socio-political infra-structure. The value of the dollar is not likely to drop by 50 percent within a few weeks, and the unemployment rate is not likely to rise to 30 percent.

Yet there are parallels between the policies of the admittedly statist-socialist Echeverria regime between 1970 and 1976 in Mexico, and the "liberal" policies which Washington has followed during the past 15 years. It is a matter of degree, not of basic philosophy and policy. On both sides of the border we find huge deficit spending to promote "full employment" and economic growth, and create a multitude of social benefits; a vast growth of the size and power of the bureaucracy; a declining value of the currency; and chronic balance of payments deficits.

What has happened in Mexico should thus be of interest to the American reader.

THE PESO CRISIS

The people of Mexico will not easily forget the shock which they experienced on the morning of September 1, 1976, when the papers informed them of the official announcement made a few hours earlier that monetary stability, to which Mexico had been accustomed for many years, had given way to "floating," which, as the people found out very soon, was merely a polite word for devaluation. Within a few days, the Mexican peso fell by 63 percent in terms of the American dollar and hard currencies.

The first shock was followed by months of uncertainty and a deepening crisis, and as 1977 progressed the Mexican people realized more and more clearly every day the crushing consequences of the inflationary euphoria of the preceding years.

What were the chief reasons for the monetary and economic crisis which overtook the country in September 1976?

There were many contributing factors, and this paper will deal only with the major ones, the varied aspects of governmental policy to cure all economic and social ills through chronic inflation.

During the 45 years between 1925, when the Bank of Mexico was established to provide a stable monetary system after years of revolutionary upheaval, and December 1970, when the Echeverria regime took over, the money supply had never exceeded 18.5 billion pesos, which it reached at the end of 1969. By August 31, 1976, the day before the devaluation — in just five years and nine months — the money in circulation had increased to 54.2 billion pesos, or by nearly 300 percent. And the printing press kept on churning out money. Between the day of the devaluation and the first of December, 1976, in just three months, the money supply rose to 77.6 billion pesos, or by another 43.16 percent. This vast increase in demand, at a time when the balance of payments showed a large deficit, and the Gross National Product grew by only about 2 per cent, as it did in 1976, largely explains the monetary crisis and Mexico's precarious economic position.

THE GROWTH OF STATISM

Moreover, the lack of monetary discipline, although the most immediate cause of the crisis, was always accompanied by other unbalancing forces, especially the tremendous growth of the government bureaucracy. In 1970, there were 247 government owned corporations and entities, in addition to twenty ministries. Six years later, at the end of Echeverria's term, the number had grown to 830, without taking into account several mixed enterprises in which the government had a direct interest.

The result of this vast expansion of the public sector was an astronomic growth of the bureaucracy and a rapid increase in the current expenditures of the government for services and salaries (as against long-term investments) which account for about 65 percent in the 1977 budget. This huge burden had to be assumed by the new government which took office in January 1977, and with no immediate increase in revenues in sight, the deficit had to be financed, at least for the time being, through more credit — and more inflation.

Since 1970 most of the government enterprises have operated in the red. While the number of government corporations increased less than four times during the six years of the Echeverria regime, the deficit increased 22 times, from 347 million to 7.4 billion pesos — and this despite the fact that government subsidies at the same time increased tenfold.

The internal and foreign indebtedness, public and private, rose rapidly to about $40 billion, which caused concern in international financial circles, including the International Monetary Fund — which nevertheless smoothed the spectacular farewell of the Echeverria regime with another $963 million loan.

The rapid expansion of overall demand during the first half of the 1970's, financed through credit expansion and with the help of the printing press, produced all the typical symptoms of an inflationary boom: expanding markets, new ventures, rising interest rates, balance of payments deficits, and a growing upward pressure on prices. In 1976 alone, the cost of living rose by 49 percent, and wages of organized labor by 52 percent.

INTERFERENCES WITH THE FREE MARKET

All this happened within a largely closed economy, which for many years had been protected by import restrictions and high tariffs, so that the powerless Mexican consumer, faced with the rapid rise of domestic prices, was unable to satisfy his needs by buying foreign goods.

Yet, despite all restrictions, the trade deficit continued to grow, reaching 74 billion pesos in 1976, which was, to a large extent, due to the failure of domestic policies especially in the agricultural sector. In Mexico, as throughout Latin American, "agrarian reforms," the distribution of land usually entail a sharp decline in the production of essential foodstuffs, with the result that, even though predominantly agricultural, these countries have to import large quantities of wheat, corn and other essentials.

While Mexican imports increased sharply, exports rose slowly, because of the rapidly rising cost of production, and the fact that most of the economic infra-structure, including the production of electricity, oil and gas, is in the hands of the government, which renders essential cost controls all but impossible.

DETERIORATING CAPITAL MARKETS

To cope with the growing imbalances at home and abroad, the government adopted a variety of fiscal measures in a vain attempt to balance revenues and expenditures. As is usually the case, virtually all the fiscal measures were directed toward squeezing more money out of the economy, while little was done to curb expenditures, which was regarded as politically inexpedient. In fact, the "fiscal reforms" consisted largely in trying to borrow more money abroad, increasing the legal borrowing capacity of the government, and creating more money.

With the government borrowing heavily in the domestic capital markets, and the markets becoming increasingly tight, the private sector looked abroad for needed capital, and the multinational corporations appealed to their home offices for funds. With interest rates at 12 and 14 percent on seemingly sound investments, and the dollar-peso rate regarded as stable, investments in Mexico appeared extremely attractive, and for years large amounts of foreign capital poured into peso loans.

And then came the devaluation, and within 72 hours the value of some $6 billion which had been invested in the Mexican economy by thousands of thrifty Mexicans and large numbers of foreign investors — many of them retired Americans who had placed their savings in seemingly lucrative — and safe — Mexican investment trusts, declined by about 50 per cent.

The hard currency reserves of the Bank of Mexico and the commercial banks shrank rapidly as maturing foreign debts were paid off and bank deposits were "dollarized." The exact figure is not known, but it is estimated that between $2.5 billion and $4 billion left the country. All this happened in a sudden crisis of confidence, the type of crisis Mexico had not known for many decades.

THE POLICIES OF STATISM

The economic policies of the Echeverria regime were dictated primarily by political considerations. As a result of the rapid expansion of government activities, the State now accounts directly, or indirectly, for about 45 percent of the Gross National Product. Every new form of public intervention was justified as being — supposedly — beneficial from a social point of view, and fair to all. Following the traditional Keynesian full employment theories, that jobs depend upon demand, demand was artificially increased by creating more and more credit and money. The Social Security System, for instance, which in 1970 covered 11 million people was expanded to cover 27 million, which quadrupled the funds needed, and once the vast bureaucratic machinery had been created, any curtailment became all but impossible.

Yet despite all the inflationary economic stimuli, unemployment continued to grow. The available statistics are not reliable, but in early 1977 the number of unemployed was estimated at six million — out of a labor force of about 18 million. And this figure tells only half the story. About 30 percent of those employed work for the government, most of them as part of the bureaucracy, and thus produce none of the basic needs of the people. Moreover, most of the unemployed —

and underemployed — are not, as in the U.S., new entrants into the labor force, but men and women who have lost their jobs. In some sectors, such as the building industry, unemployment reached 60 percent.

SIX YEARS OF STATISM AND SOCIALISM

These then are the results of the economic policies of the Echeverria regime: a high rate of inflation, economic stagnation, and a high rate of unemployment.

The flood of fiat money stimulated demand, while the government at the same time impeded production. The government tried to "distribute fairly," what the private sector had not yet been able to produce, and to tax profits which did not exist.

The devaluation of the peso was to produce vast benefits by improving Mexico's position in world markets. But since the government levied heavy taxes on exports to help finance the government deficit, and to prevent windfall profits, the promised stimulus did not materialize.

And not only the economy suffered from inflation, political activities were likewise dangerously "inflated." There were hundreds of speeches, declarations, and public demonstrations to show the people's support for the government's economic policies. Only three months before the devaluation the government undertook a costly international campaign to convince the world of the stability of the peso and the strength and rapid rate of growth of the Mexican economy. The objective was clear: to stimulate the influx of more foreign capital, both public and private, in order to finance the government's expansionist policies. And over the years the campaign was clearly successful. Mexico accumulated an external debt of about $35 billion, 70 percent consisting of public obligations, and 30 percent of the debts of the private sector.

WHAT ABOUT THE FUTURE?

The 1976 budget showed an increase of 40 percent as compared with 1975, and public expenditures continued to grow in 1977.

The large domestic and international indebtedness, both public and private, is all the more burdensome and dangerous because of the depression which overtook Mexico in 1977. Private demand fell sharply, and while the inflationary expansion of public spending during the first half of the 1970's produced an inflationary boom, a slowing down in the increase in public spending now tends to reduce private demand, and thus economic activities and employment. A government which accounts for 45 percent of the nation's Gross National Product cannot pursue a national fiscal policy, dictated primarily by the size of the tax revenues and the availability of credit. Even if the government could curb the demands of the powerful bureaucracy for more and more power and pay, the top-heavy public sector cannot be reduced freely without plunging the private sector into serious difficulties.

The private sector, moreover, faces an additional critical problem. As a result of the peso devaluation the foreign indebtedness of major enterprises has doubled, and the increased cost of servicing this debt cuts sharply into the companies' earnings, which not only reduces the income of the stockholders — and hence their ability to spend — but also the tax revenues of the government, thus making it correspondingly more difficult to balance the budget.

THE PROBLEMS OF THE NEW LOPEZ PORTILLO ADMINISTRATION

What can the new Mexican government of Lopez Portillo — what can any government in a similar situation — do to overcome the crisis and restore economic equilibrium?

The huge budget deficit which the new administration inherited is being covered in two ways — neither of which constitutes a long-range solution. Part of the deficit is financed by drawing heavily on the domestic capital market, thus making it correspondingly more difficult for the private sector to obtain needed investment funds. The rest of the deficit, it is hoped, will be financed through foreign loans secured by the income from future exports of oil and oil products.

In the meantime public investment spending was reduced sharply, or by about 25 percent during the first six months of the 1977 fiscal year, which increased unemployment and adversely affected the private sector. Thus, in addition to the acute liquidity crisis in the capital markets, those industrial and commercial enterprises which depend heavily on the public sector have slipped into a deep depression.

The government has drawn up an "administrative reform" aiming at a greater degree of decentralization, a rearrangement of functions, and a reallocation of government workers. The reform, however, failed to bring about a material reduction in the size of the bureaucracy — it was largely a question of "reallocation," although there were some isolated instance in some government corporations and agencies, where a reduction in the number of employees actually took place.

HOPE FOR THE FUTURE

Dismal as the immediate prospects appeared there was one strong ray of hope for the future: the discovery of large new oil deposits, which, it is estimated, will produce export revenues of about $23 billion between 1977 and 1982. On basis of these anticipated oil exports, the government plans to borrow $15 billion abroad to tide itself over the acute crisis.

The private sector will depend heavily upon its ability to refinance maturing foreign debts, since many of the companies do not have peso revenues adequate to meet the maturing foreign obligations which have doubled since the devaluation of the peso, and the country as a whole is faced with an acute shortage of foreign exchange.

As far as the government budget is concerned, special "excess profits" taxes have been considered to capture for the government profits resulting from what government authorities regard as "excessive" price increases on domestic sales. On the other hand, earlier plans to tax "excess profits" derived from an increase in exports due to the devaluation of the peso have been dropped.

One of the major campaign promises of the new government was an "Alliance for Production" between the government and the private sector to replace the latent hostility of the preceding six years. The Mexican economy suffers not only from obvious economic problems resulting from the policies of the Echeverria regime, but also from a basic and paralyzing lack of confidence. The country faces not only a monetary and economic crisis, but also profound psychological problems: a low state of business morale, widespread apathy, and profound distrust.

It is hard to make long-term economic plans on basis of a six year political cycle. Having been thoroughly beaten and disillusioned during the six years of the Echeverria regime, it will take time for Mexican business leaders to recover. And how long will the new spirit of "Alliance" of Lopez Portillo last?

The power of the Mexican President to establish economic policies is far greater than that of the President of the United States, where Congress, as a rule, with only two major exceptions during the past fifty years, assures a certain degree of continuity. The uncertainties of the political system that makes it difficult to project trends beyond six years, are, of course, off-set by the realization that after six years of a statist, anti-business and inflationist government, the people can vote into power a new regime which will pursue a sounder economic policy — for at least the subsequent six years.

Mexico's economic problems are essentially political in nature, and their solution must therefore be "political": a reversal of the statist-socialist tendencies of the first half of the 1970's, and a reduction of the power of the top-heavy bureaucracy, especially the top-level bureaucracy of the old regime which continues to hold on to key positions depsite the change of government.

But this is, of course, the type of problem which faces not only Mexico, but many countries throughout the free world.

XII

THE FAILURE OF "FULL EMPLOYMENT" POLICIES

G. C. Wiegand

The roots of the economic problems threatened that the United States in the 1970's — chronic inflation and unemployment — reach back to the 1930's and 1940's, to the efforts of the Roosevelt Administration to free itself from the restraints of the gold standard, and to the "full employment" philosophy of the 1940's.

THE PREMISES OF THE EMPLOYMENT ACT OF 1946

In making the President and his economic advisors responsible for achieving and maintaining "maximum employment" — a team which was never defined — Congress started with a number of basically false economic assumptions. It assumed that the "experts" could foresee the future, and that the government had the power to manipulate the course of the economy.

The White House and the Council of Economic Advisors were expected to be able to predict several months in advance, the probable level of economic activities and thus the rate of employment.

Actually no group of economic experts, let alone Congress and the bureaucracy (which has a direct stake in economic policies) is likely to agree on the future of the economy six months hence, the level of industrial production, the crop yields, the volume of exports and imports, the rate of capital formation and investments, interest rates, and the mood of the consumer. Yet all these largely unpredictable factors have a direct bearing on the level of employment.

As the Nobel prize economist Paul A. Samuelson, who is certainly more inclined toward interventionism than free enterprise, put it: "No jury of expert economists can agree on a satisfactory solution for the modern disease of stagflation." And Wassily Leontieff, who also received the Nobel prize, explained: "One reason why economists are in such disrepute is that they have pretended to understand inflation and to know how to control it, when obviously they do not." The Employment Act further assumed that the President had the power and the necessary tools to "fine-tune" the economy to prevent unemployment.

In reality, the President has no such powers, just as he is not blessed with the ability to foresee the future. An all-powerful totalitarian government may have the power — although probably not the wisdom and the economic clairvoyance — to take, virtually from today to tomorrow, the necessary fiscal, economic and monetary steps to assure certain goals — but not the President of the United States. Before the White House can put into effect any basic change in fiscal and monetary policies to "assure full employment," he must persuade Congress to adopt the necessary laws, he must convince the Federal Reserve and the American public that his policies are correct, and he must gain the cooperation of the International Monetary Fund and foreign governments and central banks.

Changes in fiscal policies, and such direct measures as price and wage controls, require Congressional action, and it may take months, if not years, to reach a political compromise that will be acceptable to the majority of the members of Congress. Changes in monetary policy require the cooperation of the Federal Reserve which may not agree with the economic forecasts of the White House.

Neither the White House nor Congress can ordinarily act quickly enough to counter cyclical changes which are likely to affect the rate of employment, even if they could predict what is likely to happen six months hence.

Ten years after the adoption of the Employment Act, the Secretary of the Treasury, George M. Humphrey warned the House Subcommittee on Economic Stabilization, that the government just cannot predict and control the course of the economy. "The most difficult situation is where you are trying to balance the effect of pressures, both inflationary and deflationary pressures, and what the effect of those pressures is going to be three months, or six months, or even some longer period hence. You are in a field where nobody can really be very sure that he is right. Worse than that . . . when you take action one way, you never will know, and nobody else will ever know, what would have happened if you had taken the action the other way." The White House and Congress are groping in the dark, and in the end often adopt policies which seem politically advisable, even though their economic effects are hard to predict.

But neither Congress nor the public like to face this truth. They are much happier if they are told that the government knows how to solve the nation's economic problems — even though past experience seems to indicate the opposite. Ten years after Treasury Secretary Humphrey warned that "we really don't know," Professor Walter Heller, the chief economic advisor to President Kennedy and President Johnson, assured the American public that we live in the "age of the economist," and that thanks to "the internal advances in recent decades . . . in economic knowledge . . . modern economics can deliver the goods."

Congress and the American public were only too anxious to accept Professor Heller's reassuring promise, yet in the subsequent decade consumer prices almost doubled, while the number of unemployed rose by 50-60 percent. The "full employment" promise had turned into the stagflation reality. The Employment Act finally assumed that the government can predict the economic, social and political consequences of a "full employment" policy in the years to come.

Washington cannot predict whether chronic deficit spending will produce full employment and prosperity (as the official economic philosophy of the postwar decades assumed) or whether it will lead to stagflation (as it actually did); what the effect of "floating" will be on the American balance of payments (few people in Washington predicted in 1971 the huge deficits of the mid-1970's); or how an increase in minimum wages will affect the chances of marginal workers to find jobs.

Nor can the government experts predict with any degree of certainty what the reaction of the people will be to socio-economic policies. It makes a great deal of difference whether the average citizen regards it as primarily his own personal responsibility to find a job and support himself and his family, or whether he has come to regard it as the responsibility of the government to provide him with a "suitable" job and an income "above the poverty level."

While it is impossible to prove the theory or to disprove it, there is a good chance that the "full employment" policies of the past thirty years actually had a tendency to increase unemployment because of their adverse effect on capital formation and thus job opportunities, and because they have tended to shift the responsibility of finding a job from the individual worker to the government.

Communist Russia has no unemployment in the American sense, but how many Americans would be willing to buy full employment by government fiat in exchange for their personal freedom — the freedom of the worker to take or not to take a job, the freedom of the entrepreneur and employer to undertake new ventures and to hire or not to hire workers, the freedom of the individual to decide how to spend or invest his money.

And that is really the ultimate choice!

THE "FULL EMPLOYMENT" PHILOSOPHY OF THE 1940's

How did the American people stumble into the "full employment" philosophy of the 1940's, and how is it possible that the nation cannot extricate itself from the web of false assumptions, despite the fact that it should be perfectly clear by this time that the full-employment-through-fiat-money-inflation has not only been a failure, but is endangering the country?

As the second World War drew to a close, the mass unemployment of the 1930's was still a vivid memory, and governments on both sides of the Atlantic, especially in Britain and the United States, were seriously concerned about the dangers of a major postwar depression.

Some eleven million American men and women were in the Armed Forces; about a third of the labor force was directly or indirectly involved in the war effort; and the returning veterans were not likely to be satisfied with a meager dole. If the American economy could produce tens of thousands of tanks and planes, why should it not be possible to produce equally large quantities of consumer goods, provide jobs for all, and assure a rising standard of living!

The theory that government intervention can assure a high level of production and employment had first been suggested by Keynes in the mid-1930's, and by the mid-1940's Sir William Beveridge's *Full Employment in a Free Society* and Henry Wallace's *Sixty Million Jobs* had become best-sellers. And both authors literally meant "full employment." As Beveridge put it: "Full employment . . . means having always more vacant jobs than unemployed men . . . The labour market should always be a sellers' market rather than a buyers' market."

To have a good job had suddenly become a "right" of every American. In his State of the Union Message in January 1944, for instance, President Roosevelt spoke of a "second bill of rights," which was to include "the right to a useful and remunerative job in the industries or shops, farms or mines of the nation."

Since then — in 35 years — the number of jobs in the United States has grown by almost 150 percent, faster than the population, and the disposable income in fixed dollars has more than trebled. America certainly did not suffer from a lack of jobs and purchasing power during the postwar decades. Yet, unemployment never dropped much below four percent except during the Korean and Vietnam wars, and during much of the 1970's it has been hovering between five and eight percent.

Why did the United States fail to solve the unemployment problem?

The pseudo-Keynesian notion that governments can create full employment through deficit spending no doubt played a role in the original wording of the Employment Act of 1946: "The rate of federal investment and expenditure may be varied to whatever extent and in whatever manner the

President may determine to be necessary for the purpose of assisting in assuring continuing full employment." These are clearly empty words. Congress and not the President controls the purse strings and determines the rate of investments and expenditures, and Congress, aside from functioning at a snail's pace, is no more blessed with economic omniscience than the White House. After a decade and a half the inherent impracticality and irrationality of the whole "full employment" policy should have been quite obvious, yet the full-employment-through-government-intervention notion did not really begin to dominate Washington thinking until the early 1960's. As Professor Heller put it in his *New Dimensions of Political Economy:* "We at last accept in fact what was accepted in law twenty years ago [in the Employment Act of 1946], namely, that the Federal government has an overarching responsibility for the nation's economic stability and growth. And we have at last unleashed fiscal and monetary policy for the aggressive pursuit of those objectives. These are profound changes. What they wrought is not the creation of a new economics, but the completion of the Keynesian Revolution."

Neither the authors of the Employment Act of 1946 nor the economic advisors of the 1960's were apparently concerned — or possibly not even aware of the fact — that economic planning by its very nature must be based on incomplete and often unpredictable data and that it is subject to uncontrolled — and largely uncontrollable — political and social forces.

The majority of politicians, from the President down, may recognize the dangers of inflation — that deficit spending financed through the Federal Reserve makes for an excess supply of money and thus higher prices; that high minimum wages hamper the employment of marginal workers; that powerful unions are likely to push up wages faster than productivity permits; that heavy taxes and welfare spending tend to increase consumption and reduce capital investments and thus production and employment, but "before an election" — and there is an election every second year — it is understandably difficult for a politician to hold down "socially desirable" expenditures, to vote against the demands of powerful unions, and to stand up against pressure groups which clamor for costly projects.

The "New Frontier" and the "Great Society" spending may have been politically expedient — total public spending increased fro $164 billion to $308 billion between 1961 and 1969 — but it was based on the false assumption that a government can create lasting prosperity and maximum employment through deficit spending and credit inflation, and it accustomed millions of Americans to the idea that Washington can provide free lunches indefinitely.

During the first half of the 1960's the "Keynesian Revolution" seemed to produce the desired results. Seven million new jobs opened up between 1961 and 1966 — and Washington claimed credit for having created the jobs; profits doubled, and the national real output rose by one-third. But while the output of goods and services increased by one-third, commercial bank credits grew by 77 percent. The country paid for the prosperity by going deeper into debt.

The inflation grew worse during the second half of the 1960's, and by the early 1970's the impact of ten years of the full-employment-through-inflation policies became only too obvious. Between the end of 1968 and the end of 1978 the consumer price index almost doubled, and internationally, in terms of hard currencies, the dollar depreciated by more than 50 percent.

THE 1946 "FULL EMPLOYMENT" DEBATE

Why did Congress fail to see in 1946 the probable

consequences of the "full employment" philosophy? Some members of Congress were no doubt aware of the potential inflationary threat. And Beveridge himself realized the danger. But he had a ready remedy: if his always-more-jobs-than-job-applicants scheme pushed up prices, wage and price controls could easily take care of the problem. Even though the title of his book called for full employment in a "free society," he was quite willing to sacrifice the free economy in order to achieve "full employment." "The list of essential liberties" he argued, "does not include the liberty of private citizens to own the means of production and to employ other citizens in operating them at a wage."

And the "Liberals" in America thought along similar lines. As one writer put it in 1946 in an article in *The Nation:* "We on the left agree with . . . the Soviet Constitution that the socialist organization of the national economy is the one certain way to guarantee full employment. We are not yet ready to state dogmatically that it is impossible to have both full employment and private enterprise . . . [but] free enterprise as it existed before the war was incompatible with full employment . . . The independent businessman will be wise to do less worrying about sacred-cow words like 'free enterprise'."

The "full employment" advocates of the 1970's are as a rule less outspoken in their advocacy of a managed socialist economy than were their predecessors in the 1940's, and some may not even realize that their policies promote such an end, but there is actually very little difference between the so-called "Leftists" of the 1940's and the so-called "Liberals" of the 1970's.

The threat of inflation, which finally overtook the country in the 1970's, was repeatedly stressed by a minority in both houses during the "Full Employment" debate, but the majority prevented any mentioning of price stability in the Act itself. As Dr. Keyserling, who became the head of the Council of Economic Advisors under President Truman, argued: "A specific statement [regarding price stability] would run the risk of causing useless controversies over the meaning of a desirable degree of price stability and of making price stability a goal that competed with the objective of maximum employment."

That was the time when Paul A. Samuelson argued that "if price increases could be held down to, say, less than five percent a year, such a mild steady inflation need not cause too much concern . . . An increase in prices is usually associated with an increase in employment. In mild inflation the wheels of industry are well lubricated and the total output goes up. Private investment is brisk, and jobs plentiful. Thus a little inflation is usually to be preferred to a little deflation. The losses to fixed-income groups are usually less than the gains to the rest of the community." This was the economic "truth" which was taught to literally millions of students throughout the world, many of whom now hold responsible and often policy-making positions.

THE EFFECTS OF "FULL EMPLOYMENT" POLICIES

What have been the actual results of this policy? Since the late 1940's the dollar has lost almost two-thirds of its domestic and an even larger share of its international purchasing power; instead of being the largest exporting nation, the United States has become one of the largest importing nations; and the rate of unemployment is materially higher today than it was during the 1940's and 1950's.

But the arguments of the "full employment" advocates have changed little during the past thirty years. "The essential idea" argued Henry Wallace in the 1940's, "is that the Federal Government is ultimately responsible for full employment," and *The New York Times* in an editorial explained that "private enterprise left to its own devices cannot provide sufficient employment." "A free economy is risky, uncertain, and inherently unstable," wrote Professor Alvin Hansen, the leading American Keynesian of the 1940's. "Thus it has at last become necessary for the government to take positive action designed to provide a stable and adequate flow of total expenditures to assure full employment."

And twenty years later, Professor Heller agreed that "the economy cannot regulate itself. We now take it for granted that the government must step in to provide the essential stability at high levels of employment and growth that the market machanism, left alone, cannot deliver."

Full-employment-by-government-fiat is, of course, possible — at least in theory — in a planned totalitarian society where workers are assigned to jobs at rates of pay determined by the government, whether the workers like the jobs or not, and whether jobs are justified or not. Given the choice between starving, being sent to a work camp, or sweeping the streets of New York at 70 cents an hour, most American unemployed, skilled or unskilled, are likely to prefer the latter form of "full employment." The Russian Constitution promises "full employment" and there is little or no unemployment in Moscow or Leningrad — but there are few American advocates of "full employment" who are willing to tell the American people plainly that to achieve "full employment," the United States should copy in many important respects the Russian socio-economic system of assigning workers to jobs the government chooses for them.

Yet there are some such advocates. In a syndicated article which appeared in the press in the fall of 1977, Robert S. Browne, the President of the Black Economic Research Center, concluded that "it is far from clear that sustained full employment is achievable without rather serious modifications of our traditional ways of doing business," including "a degree of economic planning to which Americans are unaccustomed; some degree of mandatory job assignments; government enterprise in areas traditionally felt to be the preserve of private enterprise and at least some limited control over wages and prices."

As Mr. Browne admits, "there is as yet little indication of popular support" for the remedies he suggests. Politicians do not openly recommend "planned socialism," but the country is slowly drifting in that direction from one "emergency" measure to the next.

In the end, the American people have only three choices: adopt the "full employment" system of totalitarianism; sink deeper and deeper into the chaos of inflation; or return to the pre-1930's philosophy that it is a question of "getting" a job through personal initiative, not of being "given" a job by a philosophically and financially bankrupt government.

CONCLUSION

Henry Hazlitt

Chronic large-scale unemployment is a terrible waste of economic resources. It lowers the average standard of living, and constitutes a menace to the social and political order. Every society will thus try to reduce unemployment to a minimum.

But to set up "full employment at whatever cost" as the sole, or even the chief economic goal results in a distortion and perversion of all values.[1] There are other social and economic values to be considered. In fact, in blindly trying to achieve "full employment" a country can actually destroy job opportunities and do great harm to the economic and social order in general.

As this book has shown clearly, there is wide disagreement as to what constitutes the optimum rate of employment, and there is no consensus concerning how to overcome chronic unemployment.

Yet for three decades politicians, administrators and

176

economic experts have blamed "inadequate demand" for the prevailing and gradually rising rate of unemployment. While it is no doubt true that there will not be enough jobs for all, if the consumers lack the necessary purchasing power to pay for all the goods which the economy could produce on a basis of full employment, this "lack of purchasing power" doctrine applies only under rare circumstance, and there are many other reasons which may cause unemployment: the unwillingness of the people to spend their money either because they regard prices as too high or because they fear the future; the fact that some wage rates, and especially legally fixed minimum wages, are so high that they allow little room for profit on the basis of prevailing prices; or the lack of appropriate productive facilities, because investors and entrepreneurs are reluctant to risk their money in building new factories and buying new machinery.

The attempt to attain full employment through the creation of fiat money is more likely to lead to inflation than to full employment, as the American people have learned by painful experience during the 1970's.

"Lack of demand" is rarely the chief cause of unemployment, and "demand" cannot be created out of thin air by creating more fiat money. As the supply of money increases faster than the supply of goods — between 1970 and 1977 the money stock (M2) rose by more than 90 percent while the output of goods and services rose by less than 20 percent — the purchasing power of the monetary unit, the dollar, declines, and in the end there is no more real purchasing power than there was before the government created the additional fiat money.

But in the meantime, the increase in prices, popularly referred to as "inflation," has produced a whole set of new disequilibria, and more social injustices. Yet the general public, most politicians and most economists trained in the pseudo-Keynesian tradition, fail to see that additional purchasing power can be created only through the production of additional goods and services, not through the issuance of fiat money. Inflation does not create jobs. It merely robs one segment of the population of part of its income and savings and transfers it to another segment. And this system of legalized theft gradually weakens the moral fibre of society.

THE SOCIAL AND MORAL COSTS OF "FULL EMPLOYMENT THROUGH INFLATION"

Inflation does not, and cannot "buy" full employment. In the long run it actually destroys jobs, as well as the basis of economic stability, social order and moral values. During every great inflation there has been a striking decline in both public and private morality. Let us look at three outstanding examples.

THE FRENCH ASSIGNAT INFLATION

The first is the French assignat inflation from 1790 to 1796. The moral consequences of this have been vividly depicted by Andrew Dickson White in his little book *Fiat Money Inflation in France* which grew out of a lecture he first delivered in 1876.

With prices soaring and the value of money savings rapidly diminishing, an early effect was the obliteration of thrift. Accompanying this was a cancerous increase in speculation and gambling. Stockjobbing became rife. More and more people began to see the advantages of borrowing and later paying off in depreciated money. A great debtor class grew up whose interest was to keep the inflation going. Workers, finding themselves with less and less real pay in terms of what their wages would buy, while others grew rich by gambling, began to lose interest in steady work. The evaporation of the incomes and savings of the lower and middle classes, and the sudden enrichment of speculators, with their ostentatious luxury, led to mounting social resentment and unrest. Cynicism and corruption set in. Even Mirabeau, who only a few months before had risked imprisonment and even death to establish constitutional government, began secretly receiving heavy bribes. The evidence of the general spread of corruption led to widespread distrust and a loss of faith in patriotism and virtue.

The politicians responsible for the inflation sought to throw the blame — both then as now — not only on "the speculators," but on the sellers who were forced to raise their prices. One result was that on February 28, 1793, a mob of men and women in disguise began plundering the stores and shops of Paris. At first they demanded only bread; soon they insisted on coffee, rice and sugar; and in the end they seized everything on which they could lay their hands. Hundreds of places were plundered. Finally, after six hours, order was restored, but only by a grant of seven million francs to buy off the mob. When the plundered merchants had the temerity to protest at the City Hall of Paris, they were informed that "shopkeepers were only giving back to the people what they had hitherto robbed them of."

All this was followed by forced loans, price controls, increased resort to the guillotine, repudiation of the currency, and finally the advent of the "man on horseback" — Napoleon.

THE AMERICAN CIVIL WAR INFLATION

The inflation during and after the American Civil War was far milder than the French inflation during the 1790's. Yet it was not without impact on the moral climate of the country. Emphasizing the need to return to a sound money, Hugh

McCulloch, Secretary of the Treasury from 1865 to 1868, declared in his annual report in 1867:

> "[Inflation] is corrupting the public morals. It is converting the business of the country into gambling, and seriously diminishing the labor of the country ... The kind of gambling which it produces is not confined to the stock and produce boards, but is spreading through our towns into the rural districts. Men are apparently getting rich, while morality languishes and the productive energy of this country is being diminished. Upon the demoralizing influence of an inconvertible government currency it is not necessary to enlarge ... It is not to be expected that a people will be more honest than the government under which they live, and while the government of the United States refuses to pay its notes according to their tenor, or at least so long as it fails to make proper effort to do so, it practically teaches the people the doctrine of repudiation."

THE GREAT GERMAN INFLATION

The great German hyperinflation of 1920 to 1923 followed amazingly closely the French assignat pattern. We find the same moral and social retrogression; the discouragement and final obliteration of thrift; the rise in borrowing and prodigal spending; the increase in speculation and gambling; the declining application to steady work; the wanton redistribution of income; the consequent growth of cynicism and corruption, of social unrest, bitterness and hatred, and finally of crime. But the details are worth a closer inspection.

The inflation was an unsettling and revolutionary influence. During most of its course, it lowered the real income of the workers; it improverished the old middle class of investors, and many of those who had made their fortunes from production; and it enriched a new small class of inflation profiteers whose money came from speculation. Under the appearance of feverish activity the country was producing less, and most people were poorer. Goods passed from one speculator to another, through a long chain of middlemen. Some got rich by speculating in foreign exchange; but savings-bank depositors and bondholders were all but wiped out, and even most holders of industrial securities ended with barely a fourth of their original investment. On net balance, those who profited from the inflation were successful speculators rather than producers, and certainly not the German workers; and there developed an important distinction between the new rich and old rich which had a far-reaching effect on political developments.

"It is no exaggeration to state," wrote Bresciani-Turroni, "that the depreciation of the currency caused in Germany the vastest expropriation of some classes of society that has ever been effected in time of peace." The annihilation of the value of the mark meant confiscation of the lender's wealth to the gain of the borrower. Landowners, for example, were able to free their lands from mortgage. Owners of rental properties, of course, were able to do the same, but in their case this advantage was usually more than offset by the decline in real rents, which soon did not cover even maintenance expenses, so that many owners were forced to sell or permit their properties to deteriorate.

Pensioners and others who lived on fixed incomes were reduced to abject poverty. So, in fact, were most of those in the professional and academic classes: students, tutors, writers, artists, scholars. The growing impoverishment of large segments of the population was reflected in the statistics of the condition of children — malnutrition, underweight, rickets.

The general mortality rate from pulmonary tuberculosis greatly increased between 1921 and 1923.

Property rights were in fact, not in form, obliterated. The "revaluation" decrees of February, 1924 and July, 1925 made only a paltry fractional restitution, and, of course, could not undo the millions of personal injustices and deprivations suffered while the inflation was in progress.

It is no coincidence that crimes rose sharply during the German inflation. On the basis of 1882 = 100, the crime rate, which stood at 117 in 1913, rose to 136 in 1921 and 170 in 1923. Once the inflation was over, it declined again to 122 in 1925.

TODAY'S INFLATION

What shall we say of today's conditions nearly everywhere in the world? Thanks to Keynesian ideology and spending policies, the universal abandonment of the gold standard, and the workings of the International Monetary Fund, we find a corresponding social unrest, disorder, and moral decay. The high crime rate in the United States, and terrorism throughout the world, are striking examples. Between 1960 and 1973 the crime rate in the United States increased by 120 per cent. And a similar or worse increase in crime is reported from many other countries. Another symptom of moral decay is the growing frequency of scandal and corruption in governmental circles. One of the saddest illustrations of this is Great Britain, which during most of the nineteenth and early twentieth centuries stood out among nations for the comparative integrity and incorruptibility of its civil servants and political leaders.

The chain of causation, from inflation to corruption to crime, is direct. In a free enterprise system, with an honest and stable money, there is a close link between effort and productivity, on the one hand, and economic reward, on the other.

Inflation severs this link. Reward comes to depend less and less on effort and production, and more and more on successful gambling and luck. For some, gambling finally comes to seem too chancy, and corruption and crime a surer path to quick reward.

Inflation may be sold to the people as a road to "full employment" — which, as we have seen, it is not. But by its very origin and nature, inflation must involve a redistribution of real incomes, largely to the detriment of the productive and the thrifty. The new money that the government prints goes first of all to special groups — the government officials, government contractors (and their employees), and various recipients of relief and other appropriations. As these groups spend the new paper money, they inevitably push up prices. The last to receive the new money must pay the highest prices. Those who benefit by inflation, in short, do so, and must do so, at the expense of others. The total losses through inflation must offset the total gains. This creates class or group divisions, in which the victims resent the profiteers, and in which the moderate gainers from inflation envy the bigger gainers.

Under inflation, nearly everybody is in fact being subjected to an invisible tax. For if the government in a given year spends, say, $50 billion more than it collects in visible taxes, and merely prints the rest, the public as a whole must be losing the equivalent of this $50 billion in real income. But only a handful of people realize clearly what is going on. The majority tend to blame their plight, not on the government, but on those of their neighbors who appear to be profiting from the inflation. There is a growing sense that the whole economic system has become radically unjust. "They are stealing from me, and I will steal back."

It is not merely that inflation breeds dishonesty in a nation. Inflation is itself a dishonest act on the part of the government, which sets the example for private citizens. When modern governments inflate by increasing the paper-money supply, directly or indirectly, they do in principle what kings once did when they debased the coin by adding inferior metal to the silver or gold. Diluting the money supply with paper is the moral equivalent of diluting the milk supply with water. Notwithstanding all the pious pretenses of governments that inflation is the road to full employment and prosperity, or that it is some evil visitation from without, inflation is practically always the result of deliberate governmental policy.

This was recognized by Adam Smith in *The Wealth of Nations* in a passage that bears repeating: "When national debts have once been accumulated to a certain degree, there is scarce, I believe, a single instance of their having been fairly and completely paid. The liberation of the public revenue, if it has ever been brought about at all, has always been brought about by a bankruptcy; sometimes by an avowed one, but always by a real one, though frequently by a pretended payment."

The pretended payment was inflation. The United States government today is paying off in 23-cent dollars the debts it contracted in 1940. Adam Smith went on: "The honor of a state is surely very poorly provided for, when, in order to cover the disgrace of a real bankruptcy, it has recourse to a juggling trick of this kind, so easily seen through, and at the same time so extremely pernicious."

FOOTNOTES

1. The present author has discussed this question more fully in Chapter 26, " 'Full Employment' as a Goal" in *The Failure of the New Economics*, 1959.

ABOUT THE AUTHORS

Patrick M. Boarman is President of Patrick M. Boarman Associates, International Business Consultants, Palos Verdes, California. He holds undergraduate degrees from Fordham and Columbia Universities, and the Ph.D. in economics from the Graduate Institute of International Studies, University of Geneva, Switzerland.

Dr. Boarman served as consultant to the Secretary of the Treasury, as Director of Research for the Republican Conference in the House of Representatives, and as consulting economist with a number of leading American corporations. He held professorships at Long Island and Bucknell Universities and the University of Wisconsin.

His books include *Union Monopolies and Antitrust Restraints* (1963), *Germany's Economic Dilemma* (1964), *Trade with China,* (ed., 1974), *Multinational Corporations and Governments* (ed., 1975), and *World Monetary Disorder* (ed., 1976). Boarman is also the translator of major works of the late eminent German economist, Wilhelm Roepke, including his *Economics of the Free Society* (1963).

John Chamberlain — A journalist for fifty years, he has written for *The New York Times, Fortune* and *Life* magazines, *Barron's* and the *Wall Street Journal.* For the last twelve years, Mr. Chamberlain has written an editorial page column for the King Features Syndicate which appears regularly in some 200 newspapers. His most recent books are: *The Roots of Capitalism* and *The Enterprising Americans.* The latter is now out in a new, revised edition. It deals with the business history of the United States in terms of key decisions by people — new inventions, opening up new territories, etc. Mr. Chamberlain is a 1925 graduate of Yale. Together with Henry Hazlitt and Suzanne LaFollette he started the *Freeman* magazine in 1950.

John A. Davenport — former assistant managing editor, *Fortune* magazine — was graduated from Yale in 1926. He worked for the *New York Morning World* and the Century Company before joining *Fortune's* Staff in 1937 as a writer. Editor of *Barron's National Business and Financial Weekly* from 1949-54, Mr. Davenport then returned to *Fortune* as assistant managing editor and a member of the editorial board. He retired from Time, Inc., in 1969 but continues to contribute to *Fortune, The Freeman,* and other publications. As a journalist, Mr. Davenport has written on many phases of our industrial society and has surveyed the economies of Britain, Japan, Peru and South Africa. Monetary policy and the effects of trade unions on inflation and unemployment are his specialties. He has also written on the Supreme Court and recent trends in constitutional law. The author of *The U.S. Economy,* he has been a recipient of two Freedom Foundation awards.

Henry Hazlitt — economist and author — was graduated from the College of the City of New York, and began his journalism career on the *Wall Street Journal.* At age 26 he became financial editor of the old *New York Evening Mail* and later editorial writer for the *New York Herald* and *New York Sun.* Dr. Hazlitt was literary editor of the *Sun* from 1925 to 1929, and literary editor of *The Nation* from 1930 to 1933. From 1934 to 1946 he wrote most of the economic editorials for the *New York Times* and from 1946 to 1966 wrote the "Business Tides" column for *Newsweek.* Dr. Hazlitt is the author of fifteen books, the most famous being *Economics in One Lesson,* first published in 1964 and now translated into eight languages. He also wrote *What You Should Know About Inflation, The Failure of the New Economics — An Analysis of the Keynesian Fallacies, The Foundations of Morality, The Conquest of Poverty.* He is a director CMRE.

John Q. Jennings — lawyer and labor economist — heads John Q. Jennings Associates, international economic consultants specializing in minimizing strikes and maximizing productivity. From 1941 to 1946, Mr. Jennings headed the Federal Mediation and Conciliation Service in Detroit and personally mediated the four month strike at General Motors. While serving as a consultant to the Singer Company, he started the practice of sending graphic analyses of Singer's and the U.S. Government's statistics concerning pay, profits and dividends to shareholders, employees and the general public in the many countries in which Singer operated. Among his client companies has been the British firm Guest, Keen and Nettlefelds, whose few strikes and high productivity have been noted in the Hearst newspapers, *Nation's Business,* Toronto *Financial Post,* and *Fortune.* On November 22, 1975 the *Financial Post* editorially credited Guest, Keen and Nettlefelds and Mr. Jennings with a major portion of the responsibility for the voluntary agreement by British unions to lower their demands for the nearly 35% given the striking coal miners three years previously to 10%, and a year later to 4.5%. Mr. Jennings' successful actions in Britain brought him an invitation to Australia where *The Australian* reported on January 17, 1977 that there was a 100% increase in the number of Australian corporations which are following the advice of Mr. Jennings and Prime Minister Malcolm Fraser by reporting their financial results to their employees in simple, graphic terms easily understood by all.

Donald L. Kemmerer — Professor of Economics, University of Illinois — is a specialist in American financial history. The son of an economics professor, he had his undergraduate training in economics at Princeton and his graduate training at Harvard, also in economics. He took his Ph.D. in American history at Princeton which led to his teaching career as professor in the field of American economic and financial history. He was secretary to financial advisory commissions to Chile, Poland and China. He began teaching at Lehigh University and in 1937 joined the faculty of the University of Illinois. He has been a member of the U.S. Assay Commission and has authored or co-authored six books, among them *The ABC of the Federal Reserve System* (with E. W. Kemmerer); *Comparative Economic Development* (1956, with R. H. Blodgett); *American Economic History* (with C. C. Jones) and *Path to Freedom.* Dr. Kemmerer is a member of the Mont Pelerin Society, University Professors for Academic Order, and the American Economic Association. He is one of the founders of CMRE and has been its only president.

Reed Larson — President, National Right-to-Work Committee — received an electrical engineering degree from Kansas State University in 1947 and pursued an engineering career for seven years at the Coleman Company, Wichita, Kansas. In 1958 he led the successful grassroots campaign which resulted in the adoption of a Right to Work amendment to the Kansas state constitution. Mr. Larson then became Executive Vice President of the fledgling National Right-to-Work Committee in Washington. The Committee successfully defended Section 14(b) of the Taft-Hartley Act against repeal in 1965 and 1966. In 1970 the National Right-to-Work Committee was victorious in thwarting the Nixon Administration and AFL-CIO effort to enact a law authorizing compulsory unionism in the Postal Service. Under Mr. Larson's direction the Committee has grown to over 300,000 members.

Agustin Navarro Gergely — An Economic advisor to President Lopez Portillo of Mexico is a Director of the Technical Advisory Center at the University of Mexico. His field is industrial promotion and legislation. Dr. Navarro is a member of the Ministry of Industry and Commerce and an industrial and economic advisor and consultant. He studied with Ludwig von Mises at the Foundation for Economic Education and is a member of the Mt. Pelerin Society and CMRE.

John B. Parrish — Economics Professor, University of Illinois — received his B.A. and Ph.D. from the University of Illinois. He was a research analyst for the Works Projects Administration, 1935-1936. He was a lecturer at St. Louis University and Assistant Director of Research for the United States Employment Service, St. Louis, Missouri, 1938-1939. From 1939 to 1941 Dr. Parrish was Assistant Economics Professor, Southern Illinois University and a year later was Senior Economist, National War Labor Board in Washington, D.C. He became Principal Economist to the National War Labor Board in 1942 and Regional Director of the Bureau of Labor Statistics of the U.S. Labor Department in Chicago in 1944. From 1947 to 1957 he was Associate Professor Economics, University of Illinois, becoming Professor of Economics in 1957. Dr. Parrish has served on the Education Advisory Committee of the National Association of Manufacturers and American Manpower Office, and as co-chairman, Third Annual Conference on "Careers for Women in Engineering" sponsored by the Engineering Foundation and

Society of Women Engineers. Dr. Parrish is a Ford Foundation Fellow and recipient of the Distinguished Service Award for Contributions to the Social Sciences, and of the Rodney D. Chipp Award for Distinguished Service to Women in Engineering, Society of Women Engineers. He is the author of many books and articles including *The Labor Problems of American Society*, 1952; *Problems and Policies of Dispute Settlement and Wage Stabilization During World War II*, 1950; "Business Schools and Urban Affairs: Views of 250 Leading Executives," 1970; and "Woman in Professional Training," 1975.

Hans F. Sennholz — Professor of Economics and Chairman of the Department of Economics, Grove City College — received his M.A. from Marburg University, a Ph.D. in political science from the University of Cologne, and a Ph.D. in economics from New York University. Dr. Sennholz has translated into English three volumes of Eugen von Bohm Bawerk's classic treatise, *Capital and Interest*, along with several other treatises of the same author. He is a trustee of the Foundation for Economic Education and Director of the Committee for Monetary Research and Education. Dr. Sennholz has published more than 300 essays and articles on monetary matters and other economic issues and has authored and co-authored several books, the most recent being *Gold is Money*.

G. Carl Wiegand — Professor of Economics (Emeritus), Southern Illinois University, where he taught for 18 years. He received his Ph.D. from Northwestern University in 1950. Dr. Wiegand's business career was mainly in the field of finance. He has traveled and lectured extensively in Europe, Asia, Africa and the Americas, and is the author, co-author or editor of seven books and the author of some 300 articles and monographs. Dr. Wiegand is a member of the Mont Pelerin Society, Executive Vice President of the Committee for Monetary Research, and a recipient of the Freedom Foundation Award.

Steven D. Symms — Member of Congress — received a Bachelor of Science degree in agriculture and economics from the University of Idaho. He served in the Marine Corps from 1960 to 1963, and as personnel and production manager of Symms Fruit Ranch from 1963 to his election to Congress in 1972. In 1970, he founded and published with several associates *The Idaho Compass*, a political and economic newsletter. Congressman Symms has been active in community affairs, serving as vice-president of the Marsing Chamber of Commerce and president of the Canyon County Republican Booster Club. He is a member of the Boise Chamber of Commerce and the Caldwell Rotary Club, and has served as president of the University of Idaho Alumni Association. Congressman Symms serves on the House Agricultural Committee and the Interior Committee. He is also Vice Chairman of the Republican Steering Committee. Among the many bills sponsored by Congressman Symms is HR. 427, the Jobs Creation Act of 1977, designed to accelerate private savings, investment and capital formation, thus stimulating employment.